Charitable Status
A Practical Handbook

Inter-Action Guides
Series Editor – Keith Smith

1 Battered Women and the New Law
   by Anna Coote and Tess Gill. Published jointly with NCCL.
2 Charitable Status – A Practical Handbook
   by Andrew Phillips with Keith Smith
3 Coping with the System — A Brief Citizens' Manual by Robert
   Leach. Published jointly with the National Extension College.

Andrew Phillips is a solicitor with his own firm in London, where he has specialised in piloting new, frontier charities through the hoops of registration. He was co-founder of the Legal Action Group and also of Public Interest Research Centre (Social Audit) and now acts as legal advisor to several voluntary organisations. He is a member of the Lord Chancellor's Standing Conference on Legal Services and the Political Committee of the United Nations Association.

Andrew Phillips has been active in politics for several years as a parliamentary candidate and candidate for the European Assembly. As a regular broadcaster, he is currently the 'Legal Eagle' on the Jimmy Young Show. His previous publications include: *The Living Law* (Clearway/Law Society, 1976) and *A Review of the Bingham Report* (Social Audit, 1978).

Keith Smith is the Co-ordinator of the Inter-Action Advisory Service, where he advises community groups, voluntary organisations, pressure groups and international agencies on a variety of operational matters, including charitable registration. Alongside this he works as a publisher at Inter-Action and as a trustee of Third World Publications. His other books include Marketing for Small Publishers (Inter-Action, 1980).

Charitable Status
A Practical Handbook

Andrew Phillips
with Keith Smith

Inter-Action Inprint

First published in 1980 by
Inter-Action Inprint, 15 Wilkin Street, London NW5 3NG
Second edition October 1982

Phillips, Andrew, 1939–
    Charitable status.—2nd ed.
    1. Charitable uses, trusts, and foundations
    I. Title   II. Smith, Keith, 1946–
    344.106'64   KD1487

    ISBN 0-904571-39-4

Copies available by post from the publishers, payment with order.

Trade distribution in the UK is by Southern Distribution, 17a Balfe
Street, London N1 9ED; or Scottish and Northern, 18 Granby Row,
Manchester M1 3GE; or Scottish and Northern, 48a Hamilton Place,
Edinburgh EH3 5AX.

Illustrations — Jill Fenwick

Design — John Minnion, Graham Betts and Myra Wareing

Typeset in 10/11 pt Times by
T & R Filmsetters Ltd, 77 Salusbury Road, London NW6 and
Robendene Ltd, Grimsdells Lane, Amersham, Bucks

Printed by Russell Press Ltd, Nottingham

Contents

Foreword

Basic steps to charitable status   xi

Acknowledgements

Several members of the Charity Commission have at various stages given us assistance in the preparation of this book. In particular we would like to thank Mr C A Weston, Mrs Elizabeth Cairns and Mr Samuels for their guidance. The Charity Commissioners Mr T FitzGerald and Mr T Keith have provided us with helpful encouragement. However, we must point out that this book in no way represents the official view of the Charity Commission.

A host of lawyers and advisors on charity law have provided us with information on particular points and comments on draft manuscripts. We would like to thank the following: Andrew Nicol, Ole Hansen, Antony Chapman, Adrian Longley, Harry Rajak, Malcolm Hurwitt, Francis Deutsch, Trevor Davison, G Laurence Harbottle, John M Fryer, Sue Olley, Anthony Wilson and Kevin Curley.

The Claims Division of the Inland Revenue, the Registry of Friendly Societies and the Northern Ireland Department of Finance have kindly helped us by supplying information.

We gratefully acknowledge the support and encouragement of the Barrow and Geraldine S Cadbury Trust.

We have enjoyed the forbearance of our colleagues and have benefited in particular from the comments of Hugh Craig, David Powell, Michael Collier-Bradley, Mike Jenn, Robert Grigor-Taylor, Ed Berman, Kay Knights, Kathryn Evans, Joanna Ryam, Bruce Galley, Michael Norton and Jean Jenn. We are particularly grateful to Linda Shepherd and Anne Quicke for their invaluable help in preparing the manuscript.

We hope that our efforts together with the assistance of our collaborators have produced a lucid guide for charities and those who envisage establishing charities.

The interpretation of charity law is in a continual state of flux, particularly on matters such as the payment of trustees and the limits to political action. The most up-to-date version of the Charity Commission's and court's interpretation can best be found in the Annual Reports of the Charity Commission or by writing to the Commission.

We would like to thank Stephen Lloyd for his assistance in producing this revised edition.

Andrew Phillips
Keith Smith
London, October 1979 and September 1982

Foreword

Unlucky or lucky 13

This handbook is written to try to dispel the myths about registering as a charity. Becoming a charity is neither a fuddy-duddy way of doing things nor a lucky dip. It is adopting a legal status which confers benefits on those groups wishing to help others within certain legal constraints.

The first part of this book is for anyone who wants to know what steps to take in order to qualify as a charity and thereby receive rate relief and certain tax exemptions. The step-by-step section outlines the procedure and refers you to the sections of the main text which supply the relevant details for that particular step.

The main text which follows will give charity managers and workers, solicitors, advisors, directors, trustees and donors the kind of analysis and information which few people outside the Charity Commission now possess.

As you go along you should be asking thirteen questions. Obtaining charitable status has little or nothing to do with luck. Any group can register as a charity if it is willing to fit into the current interpretation of 'charitable purposes' and if it chooses one of several acceptable legal structures through which to conduct the work of the charity.

The thirteen questions are:
1 Do you want to be a charity? Why?
2 Do you need the advantages of being one?
3 Are you aware of the disadvantages?
4 Do you need a solicitor or the help of an advisory group such as those listed under Useful Organisations at the end of this book?
5 What things do you want to do?
6 Are your activities likely to be considered 'charitable' in law?
7 Do they fit into existing very generally worded and already approved model objects clauses?

8 What structure do you want to have to run your group on a day-to-day, week-to-week basis?

9 Can you link this working constitution into a legal form like a trust or a company limited by guarantee, or even register it as an association or society?

10 Does the legal form you have selected give you the limit of liability and the all-over control you want to have for your activities?

11 Is it time to sound out the Charity Commission on your draft?

12 Have you selected trustees or directors, or do you have an electoral procedure for your association or society which satisfies you that your charity will not be split by internal strife?

13 Are you ready for a final submission to the Charity Commission to seek the quickest and surest route to charitable registration of your trust, company, association or society?

Slightly different procedures apply in Scotland and Northern Ireland and for Industrial and Provident Societies. This list of questions still applies although you will not have to register with the Charity Commission.

ED Berman

> **The following step-by-step guide is merely to give you an impression of the process of registering a charity. Do not use it as your sole guide as it is highly simplified. If, after reading it, you wish to proceed you should read the appropriate sections of the main text. You can then re-use this summary to remind yourself of the process.**

Basic steps to charitable status

1. Decide whether to become a charity.

Do not let old fashioned paternalistic overtones fool you. It is best to base your decision on the current advantages and disadvantages of becoming a charity. Chapter 1 describes these.

2. Choose a solicitor or advisory body.

This may not always be necessary. If you decide to use one consult early. Page 4 considers the issues.

3. Do your activities qualify as charitable?

The law recognises four categories of charitable activity:– relief of poverty, advancement of education, advancement of religion, some other purposes beneficial to the community. These are fairly general and embrace many activities of a socially beneficial nature. Ask yourselves whether other organisations with similar objectives to your own have registered as charities. If they have, contact them for advice. Chapter 2 covers this.

4. Prepare a constitution.

This should contain your aims (called objects) and the means of achieving them (called powers). Chapters 2 and 5 explain how to do this and advise you to use model clauses where possible. This point cannot be overemphasised. The use of generalised model clauses is the best way to try for charitable registration. Simply make sure that your particular and very special ideas fit.

At a non-legal level, although your philosophy and administration will develop from year to year, it is important that the founding group starts with a minimum agreed base as a stabilising foundation. This might cover pay, differentials and procedures for taking day-to-day management decisions etc., not all of which need to be described in your constitutional document.

5. Decide what legal format to adopt.

You can become an unincorporated organisation such as an association, society, friendly society or trust, or an incorporated organisation such as a company limited by guarantee or an Industrial and Provident Society. Unfortunately, these names have many connotations. It is best to forget these, for trusts are not only elements in wills, nor are companies merely vehicles of commercial trading. A limited company without share capital, for example, is a time honoured democratic structure. It all depends on how you use it. Chapter 5 will help you make the choice.

6. Select your charity trustees/directors.

Every charity requires trustees/directors. They are guardians of the assets of the charity. It is their duty to ensure the charity pursues its charitable aims. Chapter 6 expands on this.

7. Would the Charity Commission register you?

Ask the Charity Commission to advise you whether they would register your organisation as a charity. At this stage they should be sent your draft constitution and a statement of your proposed activities. The Charity Commission will advise you or your solicitor, though you may have to undertake a fairly prolonged correspondence with them. Procedures for this step are different for charities in Scotland and Northern Ireland and for Industrial and Provident Societies. See chapter 4.

8. Formalise your constitution.

Once you have received the go-ahead from the Charity Commission or Inland Revenue, finalise your constitution, with any suggested amendments and formally adopt it by completing the appropriate documents.

9. Register as a charity.

Send the Charity Commission two copies of your adopted constitution with a completed Application for Registration as a Charity (RE1). This step is not required of charities in Scotland and Northern Ireland or of Industrial and Provident Societies.

10. Start or return to your real work.

In due course you will receive your registered charity number and a statement confirming your charitable status from the Charity Commission. Chapters 7 and 8 describe what a charity can and cannot do.

11. Check your financial management system.

The Charity Commission and other bodies will usually require you to submit annual accounts. Ensure you have a system that allows you to do this easily and accurately and that allows your organisation to keep in touch with its financial state of health day by day. Chapter 9 outlines the tax relief a charity is entitled to receive.

1 Why become a charity

Over 1700 new charities are set up and registered each year. Very few of these are large national organisations such as Oxfam or Help the Aged; most are small groups active at grass-roots level.

Even if you are only one of a small band of friends working on

The charity label is useful in the hunt for funds.

a common cause during the evenings, it might be worth your while to register your organisation as a charity.

The major advantages

Fund-raising

The public will be reassured if you are a registered charity. Although you may not envisage shaking collecting tins on street corners, you may well want to appeal to local traders for free goods, whether it be timber for building, off-cuts for play materials or even food to see you through the early days. 'We are a charity . . .' can be a useful label in this hunt.

But more important than public appeals are those requests made to existing sources of finance for voluntary bodies. Most of these are charitable foundations. They, like the public, are bombarded with requests for grants. Many of them are prevented by the terms of their constitutions from making grants other than to charitable organisations, but many more are inclined to operate an internal rule of thumb cutting out all applicants which are not registered as charities. This first winnowing may be crude, but it is a fact of life in the voluntary field.

Rate relief: mandatory and discretionary

You will automatically be entitled to rate relief of at least 50% on the premises occupied by the charity, ('mandatory rate relief'). Your group may not occupy any premises yet but if you do, you will know how crippling rate bills can be.

Your local authority also has the discretion to grant up to 100% rate relief to charities, though most authorities, especially those in southern England, are reluctant to go that far. If you want to obtain this further relief, see your local rating officer. Discuss the factors which will weigh most heavily with the council in considering any application. See page 65 for details.

Tax advantages

In general, the tax advantages for charities have become increasingly important in recent years. This is not only because new taxes have been introduced, but also because of the increase in taxation rates especially for traditional individual donors. This has meant, firstly, that there has been relatively less money available for charitable gifts. Secondly the donor, while receiving no direct financial benefit, will often get some incentive from being able to

2

give in a way which sees the tax element go to the charity rather than to the State.

The taxes concerned are as follows:

Income Tax – on personal incomes
Corporation Tax – on company profits
Stamp Duty – on the value of property transferred
Rates – on property rateable values
Capital Transfer Tax – on gifts and property passing on death
Capital Gains Tax – on capital profits on property disposals
Value Added Tax – on sales of goods and services
Development Land Tax – on planning consent values
National Insurance – no surcharge

The taxation system is complex and has been changing rapidly in recent years. The particular advantages that are available to charities at the current time for each of these taxes are given in some detail in chapter 9.

The disadvantages of becoming a charity

Probably the most frequently experienced draw-back of registering as a charity are the limitations the law then places on certain forms of political and campaigning activities. If you expect this restriction to interfere with your activities, check chapter 7.

3

2 Becoming a charity

Using solicitors

There is a time to seek the advice of the expert, just as there is a time to paddle one's own canoe. When in doubt consult someone with experience of your situation, such as another charity.

If you decide to use a solicitor look for one who is reasonably experienced in handling charity formations of the kind you are involved with. There are not all that many solicitors whose practices embrace much first hand involvement with some of the newer types of charities such as community groups, self-help organisations and participative charities. All you can do is to seek recommendation from a variety of informed sources – other charities in the same field; grant giving foundations; advisory services and perhaps best of all from solicitors you may know and who will recommend a solicitor experienced in the charity field.

The first thing you will need to establish in going to a solicitor is what they can do for you and at what cost. The tendency of many organisations is to skimp setting-up costs, if only because until they are set up they are likely to be extremely short of funds. However, this can prove to be a false economy. Not only will the inexperienced solicitor tend to give inexperienced advice, but the time it can take to obtain registration, can more than outweigh any cost advantage. Quite apart from this if a less conventional charity fluffs an application for registration, it can make a second attempt a much more difficult undertaking.

At your first meeting with your chosen solicitor you should find out:

(a)   Roughly speaking, what hourly rate they will charge you. To give you a very rough idea, a middle ranking partner of a provincial firm will charge time at £30 per hour in 1982. However, many solicitors moderate their charges for charities.

(b) Roughly speaking, how many hours do they expect to spend advising upon, or drafting, the constitution for your proposed charity or advising on any other matters related thereto. Are they going to use model 'objects' clauses and other model parts of constitutions already approved by the Charity Commission or the Inland Revenue?

(c) What priority can they give your work?

(d) Roughly how long do they expect each stage of the formation and registration to take?

(e) What part of the work involved in formation and registration do they think you could usefully do yourself, or assist them in doing? A word of warning here – to go to solicitors with your own attempts at a draft constitution and require them to work from that can cause more problems than it solves.

The important thing is to instruct a solicitor you have confidence in and can get along with, and then trust him or her to do a reasonable job in a fair way. Most solicitors respond much better to this sort of relationship than one which is over-regulated by the client. Tell them what you want to do and how you want to do it, in plain English. They will soon translate it into the appropriate jargon.

Even if it is appropriate for you to take over another charity's rules lock, stock and barrel, it may still be advantageous to work with and through a solicitor. The Charity Commission seem to be more relaxed if the application and correspondence is routed through a solicitor.

There are several agencies that are experienced in advising groups how to register such as the Civic Trust, the National Council for Voluntary Organisations, the National Federation of Housing Associations and the Inter-Action Advisory Service. Several of them are described in this guide, under Useful Organisations. Others will be known in your particular field.

What you should do, in any event, is to obtain from another charity in your field, operating as near as possible to the way you would like to operate, a copy of its constitution. This can serve as a guide to you and your solicitor or advisor. If that is not possible, you have the right to search the public files of the Charity Commission.

These files of constitutions, or 'governing instruments' as the Charity Commission call them, are indexed alphabetically and by area and also by type of charity. See Charity Commission in the Useful Organisations section of this book.

What is 'charitable'?

It is not enough for your group merely to be doing things you consider worthwhile to be sure of obtaining charitable status. The legal definition of a charity is still derived from the preamble to an Elizabethan Act of Parliament of 1601, redefined in 1891 under four heads by Lord Macnaghten. To become a charity you will have to satisfy the Charity Commission in England and Wales or the Inland Revenue in Scotland and Northern Ireland that the purposes or objects of your organisation fall *entirely* under one or more of these heads of charity.

The four heads of charity

The four heads of charity are:
 (1) the relief of poverty
 (2) the advancement of education
 (3) the advancement of religion
 (4) other purposes beneficial to the community
The fourth head has a limited meaning so consult page 13 before settling for it.

Objects clause

The purposes for which any organisation exists are normally set out in what is called its objects clause in its constitution. The objects are obviously of fundamental importance, for they describe the goals and areas of concern of the organisation. All its activities will have to come within the limits described in the objects clause, for otherwise they will be unauthorised (or, as lawyers say, ultra vires). Above all, the objects must fall entirely within one or more of the four charitable categories in order for registration as a charity to be obtained.

While the Charity Commission will be most interested in your statement of objects, they will also probably want to know of your intended activities, to determine whether they are likely to come within your defined objects. For these reasons you must draft your objects clause carefully and cautiously. Where possible, adopt the objects clause of a registered charity which is engaged in similar activities to your own or adopt one of the model clauses. If you tell the Charity Commission that you have adopted a model, it should make your passage through the Commission quicker and smoother.

It is vital to draft your objects clause correctly the first time. This is the moment to obtain expert advice if you are unsure of your ground. Although you can resubmit a draft constitution with entirely changed objects, after rejection of the first draft by the Commission, this may well incline the Commission to think either that you don't know what you are doing, or that you are disguising your real and uncharitable objects behind a charitable facade.

Timing

It is also easier for a group that is still forming and constituting itself to register as a charity than one that is established. Therefore if you decide that it would be to your group's advantage to have charitable status later on, you should consider registering as a charity while you are establishing your constitution. That is to say, do this before the press has written about your activities. Publicity material and press reports can distort the activities of your group and give the Charity Commission a false idea of your purposes.

Registration as a charity can take from eight weeks to two years depending on whether the proposed charity is clearly charitable or has purposes which are more borderline. The following chapters should help you to keep the process as brief as possible.

It is most important that in the first instance you send your *draft* constitution, before you formally adopt it, to the Charity Commission for their comment. (If you are located in Scotland or Northern Ireland, the Charity Division of the Inland Revenue rather than the Charity Commission will give you this advice.) Only after it has been agreed by the relevant authority that your organisation would be charitable should you adopt your constitution. If you are located in England and Wales you must then formally register with the Charity Commission, unless your organisation is exempt as described on page 22.

If, however, you have to establish your organisation before Charity Commission approval has been obtained, make sure that your constitution expressly allows any amendment to be made for the purposes of achieving charitable status.

Fees

No fees are charged by either the Charity Commission or the Inland Revenue. But bear in mind that you may have solicitor's fees and a registration fee if you incorporate as a company or Industrial and Provident Society. We describe this in chapter 5.

The first head – the relief of poverty . . .

There is no neat definition of poverty

The meaning of the term 'poverty' is relative and varies from age to age, so that today there are several definitions which command respect. Above all to count as poor people do not have to be destitute. In practice the persons to be benefited by the organisation applying for registration as a charity would have to be clearly outside all of the current definitions of poverty before the Charity Commissioners are likely to refuse registration on these grounds.

Poverty charities can be restricted in benefit

Poverty charities are the only ones which will be accepted for registration even if they are providing benefit to only a small group of connected people. Charities registered under the other three heads must provide benefit to the public at large, or a substantial proportion of the public. Thus, for example, an organisation set up to relieve the poverty of necessitous employees and ex-employees of a specified firm is charitable. But an organisation set up to advance the education of the employees and ex-employees of a specified firm (second head) would not qualify as charitable.

The first head also covers relief of the 'impotent' and the 'aged'. The word impotent is nowadays usually taken to mean the sick, handicapped or mentally ill. The modern view is that the impotent and aged beneficiaries need not be poor.

Relief can be indirect

It is also enough for the relief of poverty, in a charitable sense, to be achieved by indirect means. This might be by providing travel facilities to enable hard-up relatives of prisoners to visit them. Or it could mean the provision of basic equipment or expertise whereby 'poor' people might be enabled to rise above their poverty. This might be achieved, for instance, by supplying machinery for home industries in the under-developed world.

8

The relief of poverty in any part of the world.

Poverty charities can have generalised objects

Generally speaking it will be found that the Charity Commissioners are less worried by applications on behalf of poverty charities than by those of the other categories. This is why the drafting of objects for this type of charity can be very straight-forward, and the Commissioners are usually content with extremely generalised wording.

In the past, the Courts have accepted under the poverty category such generalised beneficiaries as *persons of moderate or limited means* or *those who are not self-supporting* or *poor struggling youths of merit* or *debtors* or *indigent single people who have shown sympathy with science*. A simple object such as the *relief of poverty anywhere in the world* has also been acceptable.

Example 'relief of poverty' objects clause

The objects clause of a charity for relief of poverty at home and abroad might read: 'To relieve poverty in any part of the world' or for a local charity 'to relieve poverty in Charityville'.

See Further Reading for *Charities for the Relief of the Poor* and *Charities for the Relief of Sickness.*

The second head – the advancement of education

A widely interpreted and developing category, it is probably the most extensively used for the creation of dynamic charities today. As with 'poverty' there is no hard and fast definition of what constitutes 'education'. So long as an intelligent and responsible case can be made out to the Commissioners, new branches of teaching and learning should find acceptance for charitable status.

'Education' is fortunately interpreted widely and not confined to conventional academic teaching. The promotion of commercial education has long been looked upon as charitable, as has the teaching of principles of 'discipline, loyalty and good citizenship' which is one of the objects of the Scouts.

Sporting facilities and teaching aids are charitable

The definition of education in a charitable sense extends to the promotion of physical education such as the provision of sports facilities. But see page 20. It also extends to the provision of facilities which enable teaching to be more effective such as libraries, projectors or the running of training courses.

Education in culture and the arts

Aesthetic education in culture and the arts is an expanding field within the education category. The law takes a liberal view of what is permissible in this area, and with careful preparation you should not experience too much difficulty in establishing a charity for the promotion of aesthetic education. For example a choir has registered by giving its objects as 'to promote the practice and performance of choral works' and organisations staging concerts and drama have registered.

In their report for 1977 the Charity Commissioners noted an upsurge in the number of theatre groups registering. Community arts organisations such as street theatre troupes, which can justify charitable status on education grounds, are acceptable to the Charity Commission provided that they are not evidently advocating a cause.

However, 'mere entertainment' or 'artistic purposes' have

10

been held by the Courts to be too wide and vague. Whereas an artistic pursuit which is described in the objects of the organisation seeking registration as 'cultural' or 'classical' is perfectly acceptable and has the full backing of precedent. These distinctions are bemusing but they are the law.

Education and public benefit

Charitable education need not be restricted to the poor. Eton is a charity school. But the possibility of benefit to the community or a substantial section of it is essential.

Research activities are generally charitable although, again, they must be of public benefit. In practice this test is usually satisfied by placing the trustees under a duty to disseminate the results of the research by teaching or publication or, at least, to make the research available to the public on a come-and-get-it basis. It may even be enough if the research is of significant educational value to the researcher and indirectly through him or her to the public, though plainly sole reliance on this claim will tend to invite scepticism.

Occasionally one must confront the argument that a particular organisation in the education field is not entitled to charitable status because its work, although available to the public, is not 'beneficial'. Thus, to take an extreme case, the Courts would not accept as charitable an organisation to educate the young in pornography. 'Teaching' or 'education' has on occasion been distinguished by Judges from a simple 'increase of knowledge'.

A case falling the wrong side of this line was the one involving the Will of George Bernard Shaw where it was held that the Trust he established by his Will, whose object was development of a new alphabet, was not charitable. Another case in 1967 involved a 'museum' gift which failed because it had no educational or public utility amounting, in the words of the Judge, to no more than 'foisting on the public a mass of junk'.

Some political education can be charitable

The Courts have objected to organisations which propose to operate, or in fact operate, as the propaganda arms of related political groups or parties. By contrast, it has long been accepted that education about politics in the academic sense is acceptable, as is education in political principles. The dividing line between what is allowed and what is not is indistinct and gives rise to much argument and room for value judgement.

11

In practice, success or failure in an application for registration of an organisation whose activities are likely to be in or on the edge of politics will depend to a great extent on the confidence which the Charity Commissioners have in the applicants and their preparatory work. For further discussion of politics and charity law see chapter 7.

Example 'advancement of education' objects clause

A simple modern constitution to establish a charity which could operate generally in the education field might have an objects clause as follows: 'To advance education in the United Kingdom for the public benefit'.

However the Charity Commission tend to dislike such wide objects and would probably seek to narrow them down. But if you can show that your potential activities may extend to a wide range of education activities, you should win the argument.

By contrast, the objects of the local playgroup where the sponsors have no wider ambitions would adequately be defined as: 'To provide educational facilities for under-sixes in the town of Charityville'.

The third head – the advancement of religion

'Religion' is not confined to Christian sects

'Religion' includes any form of monotheistic religion though it is likely that established religions have an easier passage in registering. However, the so called non-religious or ethical societies based on humanism are not deemed religious charities but may be eligible for registration as either educational charities or as charities established for purposes beneficial to the community.

There must be an outgoing benefit to the public

In a case in 1949 the Court decided that a gift for an order of enclosed, contemplative nuns was not charitable because, although plainly a religious gift, it lacked that outgoing element of advancement (i.e. instruction or edification of the public) which is essential. In reaching this decision the Court refused to accept the efficacy to the public of the intercessory prayers of the nuns.

Example 'advancement of religion' objects clause

On the assumption that those establishing the trust were interested in propagating Christian principles, the object clause at its simplest might read as follows: 'To propagate Christian principles for the benefit of the public anywhere in the world'.

The fourth head – other purposes beneficial to the community

The 'other purposes' are those outside the poverty, education and religion heads but within the so called 'spirit and intendment' of the 1601 Preamble. However, before anyone should think that this offers a bandwagon for all good causes, it is fair to point out that 'other purposes' are not 'all other purposes' but only those beneficial to the community (or a substantial part of it) in a way which is recognised as such by law. Thus the fourth category is by no means as free and wide as might first appear.

But it does give some elbow room in which to extend charitable frontiers and as such this category has a potentially dynamic dimension which the others tend to lack. On the other hand, one must not forget that all definitions have a degree of elasticity which, given imaginative advocates and bold Judges, permits extension of concepts in the other three categories so as to respond to broad social and cultural developments in our society.

Community benefit and some examples

In the most general terms this category includes objects of 'general public utility' such as funds for public works or for the relief of public burdens. It also allows objects of 'moral improvement'. Examples of the objects of charities within this category have included: the protection of lives or property of the community; preservation of public order; resettlement and rehabilitation of servicemen or prisoners; disaster funds; public relief from taxes or rates; promotion of industry, commerce and art; promotion of public recreation; national or local defence; promotion of moral welfare.

Animal charities fall under this head but are only charitable if their object is to benefit the *human* public. They can for instance be set up to protect public morality by preventing cruelty to animals.

Many of these objects overlap into one or other of the three categories already mentioned, so giving the applicants for charitable status two or more strings to their bow.

The provision of recreational and leisure facilities

The Recreational Charities Act 1958 was intended to make it clear that it was charitable 'to provide, or assist in the provision of, facilities for recreation or other leisure-time occupation, if the facilities are provided in the interests of social welfare'.

13

The registration of sports groups as charities is problematic at the moment. Sport merely for entertainment is not charitable. Details are given on page 20.

*Animal charities are only charitable if their object is to benefit the **human** public.*

Example 'other purposes' objects clause

There is no typical objects clause for this fourth category of charities, since it is of such a wide-ranging scope. The Charity Commissioners will in suitable cases allow objects stated simply in terms of being 'to relieve poverty advance religion promote education and to do all such other things beneficial to the community as may be charitable under the laws of England and Wales' or 'for the general benefit of the inhabitants of Charityville'.

Charitable activities

The Charity Commission will not be concerned only with the objects clause. They are also likely to ask you for a description of your intended *activities* to see if they would be charitable by law. Your statement of these requires care and accuracy but this guide will help you in this.

What is 'public benefit'?

A charity, other than some poverty charities, must benefit the whole community or a sufficiently large or important section of it. As with many other of the tests, it is sometimes difficult to know just what is a sufficient section of the community to fulfil this requirement. But it is clear that clubs which exist merely for the benefit of members are unlikely to be charitable unless the only membership restriction is a geographical one such as 'for the inhabitants of Charityville'. It is also clear that sufficiency in this context can be qualitative or quantitative. For example, a charitable trust to advance education in an obscure branch of physics would not be ruled out because there were only a handful of potential students.

Foreign publics

It is perfectly acceptable for a charity in one or other of the first three categories to have as its object benefit of a foreign public. It is doubtful whether this is so in respect of the fourth category.

What is 'public benefit'?

This question is only likely to arise under the fourth head of 'other purposes beneficial to the community'. See page 13.

On rare occasions the question intrudes on the other heads such as when a sceptical House of Lords considered the prayers of the nuns lacked efficacy. Similarly, as we have already seen the promotion of sport has been held not to necessarily involve benefit.

A charity must have exclusively charitable objects

A charity can only be registered as such if its objects are exclusively charitable. That is to say all its purposes must be charitable on any reading of the words used. Occasionally this gives rise to difficulties. Generally speaking it is safer when drafting the objects to link descriptive adjectives by the word 'and' as opposed to the word 'or' so as to require a conjunctive rather than a disjunctive construction.

The importance of this was vividly illustrated by a case in 1885. There the Court held that 'charitable and deserving' objects were exclusively charitable although, had the words been 'charitable or deserving' they would not have been. Upon analysis, the reason for this is clear. For although what is 'charitable' must be 'deserving', the reverse is not necessarily so. Some causes which might be deemed deserving might not be charitable.

15

This does not of course prevent you drawing up an objects clause which refers to several heads of charity. In fact it is a positive advantage to do so if you want to have the freedom to be flexible in a changing society. For example, many Citizens Advice Bureaux have the following simple objects clause:

> The Bureau is established for the purpose of benefiting the community in Charityville and surrounding area (a) by advancing the education of the public in matters relating to mental, physical and social welfare (b) by relieving poverty.

Dissolution clause

The power to dissolve

Whatever form a charity takes its constitution ought to provide for it to be wound up in certain circumstances. The circumstances might depend upon the wishes of the promoters. It is quite common to make an arrangement whereby all the trustees, or three-quarters of the members of a charitable company voting on the matter, have the authority to dissolve the charity. In the case of associations such as charitable community associations the power may be cast wider.

Surplus assets on dissolution

It is essential that a dissolution clause states what should be done with any surplus left on dissolution, after all the obligations of the charity have been paid off. The law requires that it should go to another charity, or for charitable purposes. Otherwise monies which have been donated to the charity could find their way to non-charitable causes on dissolution. Usually the trustees of a charity will distribute all the assets before dissolution, but if they do not the constitution should provide specifically or generally for what should then occur. Often the arrangement is that the surplus goes to another charity operating in a similar field chosen by the majority of the trustees. Sometimes that charity is actually named in the dissolution clause. Sometimes discretion is left completely to the trustees to exercise at the time. The following clause is one example:

> . . . the assets of the charity (if any) after payment thereout of all proper debts and liabilities should not be paid or distributed amongst the members but shall be given to such other charitable organisation or organisations with objects similar to those of the charity as the members for the time being shall decide or in default of any such decision as shall be decided by the committee (all such decisions to be by simple majority).

It is emphasised that this wording may not be suitable to your particular circumstances.

3 Some newer types of charity

Over the last few years certain categories of groups have encountered special difficulties in obtaining charitable status. The following sections describe current law and policy as it refers to some of them.

Self-help

The most common form of mutual self-help groups are those established by and for the sufferers from a disability and those established for health care. Alcoholics Anonymous are one of the best known groups of this type. If such groups are set up and run by a closed group of people merely for their own benefit they would not be charitable however worthy their aims. But they can qualify as a charity if their objects are for the public benefit (i.e. are not restricted to the members of the organisation) by being available to all those people (nationally or locally) who are suffering from the disability.

Another category of self-help group is neighbourhood and community associations. For such organisations model charitable constitutions exist which accord substantial control of the organisation to those inhabitants of the area who belong to the organisation. The simpler model is available from the Scottish Council of Social Service and a longer one from the National Federation of Community Associations (see Useful Organisations).

Housing Associations

Certain Housing Associations are also acceptable in principle for charitable status. Most Housing Associations now register under the Industrial and Provident Societies Act. The National Federation of Housing Associations have agreed several sets of model rules with the Registrar of Friendly Societies. One set (Model H. 13 1977) establishes an association with charitable status. The NHFA describe this model as 'suitable for associations formed by social, religious and similar groups for the provision of accommodation for persons in necessitous circumstances, e.g. the relief of poverty, general family housing among the lower income groups, as well as the elderly and the disabled'. Further information and advice is available from the NFHA (see Useful Organisations).

Advice giving

Some organisations have encountered difficulties in obtaining registration with advice-giving objects. However, if you can clearly show that such advice is educational and/or will be instrumental in relieving poverty, registration will be obtained. Some law centres, for example, have registered in the last few years with amongst their objects 'to provide free legal advice and assistance to persons resident in Charityville. . .'.

The Charity Commission can become anxious where advice services are available to the well-off in a borough. One way of avoiding means-testing your clients may be to show that your advice-giving is primarily advancing education. Another situation in which means-testing is unnecessary is where the *nature* of the advice being given implicitly excludes those who are not 'poor'.

Unconventional medicine and therapy groups

In 1975 the Charity Commission decided that institutions promoting fringe medicine or therapy would have to satisfy them that the treatment has some merit. Evidence is unlikely to be required from institutions practising activities such as acupuncture, osteopathy or faith-healing but will be required from those practising less well known forms of treatment. This evidence could take the form of case studies or indications that the treatment or therapy is acceptable to at least a sector of the 'medical profession'.

Ethnic organisations

A group set up to relieve poverty, advance education or pursue other charitable purposes among people of a certain racial group such as Jews, Irish or West Indians is lawful and can obtain charitable status provided benefits are not restricted by reference to colour. An acceptable phrase to describe, for example, second generation immigrants is 'people of West Indian ethnic origin.'

'Promoting good race-relations' as such is surprisingly not of itself considered charitable. Thus an organisation promoting through its newsletter a favourable attitude towards multi-racial living as experienced in mixed marriages was refused registration in 1978. One way around this problem is to define objectives in terms of 'the advancement of education in good citizenship'. This is a phrase acceptable to the Charity Commission and comes very close to encompassing all the activities of many organisations in the race relations field.

If you require further advice on registering a race relations or ethnic group you can contact the Legal Department of the Commission for Racial Equality (see Useful Organisations). Local Community Relations Councils are invariably registered as charitable, and their objects are a useful source of ideas.

Employment projects

Training for the relief of unemployment has been charitable since 'support, aid and help of young tradesmen, handicraftsmen and persons decayed' was so designated in 1601. But there is an important distinction between an organisation which provides job training (i.e. education) and one which simply provides employment. The former is charitable; the second is not. The major difficulty which arises for some job creation projects is that if they provide both training and employment, the claim can be made that their purposes are not exclusively charitable and therefore that they cannot register as charitable. Although problematic, several possibilities are open in these cases.

Recent rulings by the Charity Commission state that they will refer to the rate of turnover of trainees in determining whether the purposes of the organisation are the provision of training or the provision of employment. Indications are that Manpower Service Commission projects where there is an annual turnover of trainees will therefore be viewed as educational. Another possibility may be to show that your organisation is promoting the development of industry or commerce in general, which is a charitable purpose under the second head. A third possibility is to split your operation into two parts so as to hive off the non-charitable workshop element to trade freely, e.g. repairing vehicles at commercial rates. This leaves the training element to operate as an educational charity.

19

Where the work done by your trainees is in itself charitable, such as relieving the poverty of others or undertaking environmental improvement, there is no problem. A group of this type registered recently with the following as part of its objects clause:

(1) To further the education and training of unemployed persons, and in particular young persons, by providing them with opportunities for work in the field of social and community service, and by arranging educational courses for them.

(2) To relieve need among such persons by providing them with paid employment.

Details of the most recent rulings and advice for MSC and other job creation projects wanting to register as charities are available from the Community Schemes Unit of the National Council for Voluntary Organisations (see Useful Organisations).

Sporting facilities

Most people tend to think that sports clubs and associations should be entitled to charitable status. However, this is not the case where the organisation has restricted membership. Restriction in this sense more usually relates to a limitation of the facilities concerned – usually a playing field and clubhouse – to one particular sport. The requirement that those who use the facilities shall pay some sort of fee or subscription is not considered a restriction in this sense, unless it is plainly of an amount that is meant to operate as an effective veto on the bulk of the public.

The law in this area is in a state of remarkable uncertainty. What seems clear, however, as the Recreational Charities Act 1958 was designed to clarify, is that provision of facilities for recreation or other leisure time occupation provided in the interest of social welfare (i.e. improving the conditions of life of those affected) for either the public at large or any disadvantaged group (which includes both the old and the young) will be charitable. It is under this heading that village halls and women's institutes, for example, are registered. While uncertainty continues it is unwise to use the word 'sport' in your constitution. The term 'recreation' is much more acceptable.

A recent model approved by the Inland Revenue and Charity Commission as charitable reads as follows:

(1) The object of the Association shall be the provision in the interests of social welfare of facilities for recreation and other leisure-time occupations for the inhabitants of Charityville being facilities,

    (a) of which those persons have need by reason of their youth, age, infirmity or disablement, poverty or social and economic circumstances; and

    (b) which will improve the conditions of life for such persons by promoting their physical, mental and spiritual well-being.

In order to show that the facility is a provision in the interests of social welfare and that it will improve the conditions of life, some deprivation must exist. This does not need to be great and the mere fact that the facility does not exist locally is likely to be sufficient.

Disaster appeals

Following the confusion that arose over the nature of the Penlee lifeboat disaster fund, the Attorney General has issued a Statement on Disaster Appeals. You can obtain copies of this from the Charity Commission, the Attorney General's Office or through your bank, local authority or lawyer.

If you set up an appeal following a disaster or accident or when an individual's suffering moves people to give, you should make it clear to donors from the start whether the fund is charitable or not. A charitable fund attracts tax relief which swells the size of the fund but it cannot be used "to give individuals benefit over and above those appropriate to their *needs*". If your appeal is to be a charity, you should make it clear in the appeal what any surplus funds will be used for. The Attorney General suggests the following form:

This appeal is to set up a charitable fund to relieve distress caused by the accident/disaster at   on
The aim is to use the funds to relieve those who may be in need of help (whether now or in the future) as a result of this tragedy in accordance with charity law. Any surplus after their needs have been met will be used for charitable purposes designed: (i) to help those who suffer in similar tragedies (ii) to benefit charities with related purposes (iii) to help the locality.

If you decide to use a more striking form of words, be sure that it is unambiguous.

4 Other aspects of registration

As we have explained most new charities are required to register with the Charity Commission. This section explains the exceptions to this and the variations and difficulties that may be encountered in the course of registration.

Exempt charities

Some charities have been accorded the privilege of being exempt from some of the administrative provisions of the Charities Act. So they do not have to register with the Charity Commission, nor submit annual accounts to the Charity Commission, nor can the Commission conduct inquiries into their activities. The main general exceptions encountered are:

— any charitable society registered under the Industrial and Provident Societies Act or the Friendly Societies Act
— voluntary schools
— the Boy Scouts and Girl Guides
— Baptist, Congregational and other churches
— Church of England Bodies and places of worship
— small charities meaning those neither having any permanent endowment or investment or rental income of over £15 per year, nor in occupation of any property. If you are in doubt about whether your organisation is small enough not to register, then ask the Charity Commission for advice.

Scotland

The principles of registration, as we have explained them, apply to organisations based in Scotland when they apply for charitable status, except that the Charity Commission's remit does not cover Scotland. Therefore, prospective charities should send their draft constitution and a copy of their latest accounts (if any) to their local Inspector of Taxes. Once this has the Inspector's approval, submit a certified true copy of your constitution, as finally approved, to the Inspector and you should receive a letter from the Inland Revenue in Edinburgh establishing your charitable status.

There is no register of charities in Scotland. Advice on charitable registration can be obtained from the Scottish Council of Social Service (see Useful Organisations).

Northern Ireland

Northern Ireland is similar to Scotland in that it is beyond the remit of the Charity Commission but the same definitions of charity pertain.

An organisation based in Northern Ireland should draw up its draft governing instrument, as we have outlined. But you should then submit it to the Charity Division of the Inland Revenue in Bootle (see Useful Organisations) for their opinion on whether or not the organisation would qualify as charitable for tax purposes.

Under the Charities Act (Northern Ireland) 1964 the Charities Branch of the Northern Ireland Department of Finance was given many similar functions (but not registration) to those of the Charity Commission for England and Wales, but with restricted powers. They will, for instance, give advice to charities and prospective charities.

Charities in Northern Ireland are exempt from rates, for details see page 66.

The Inland Revenue

During the process of vetting a prospective charity, the Charity Commission consult the Inland Revenue unless the applicant clearly falls within one of the established charitable precedents.

Since the Inland Revenue stand to lose more tax revenue each time a new charity is registered, they tend to be tough on applicants. Sometimes, therefore, the Charity Commission will argue with the

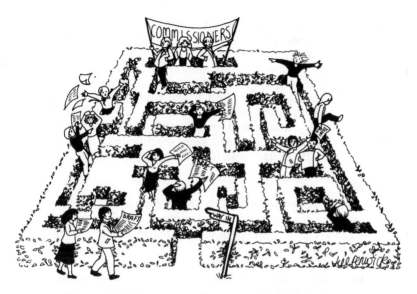

It can be difficult to get to speak to the person who ...

Inland Revenue in favour of granting charitable status. The Charity Commission may suggest alterations in draft constitutions to the applicant to overcome objections that have been lodged by the Inland Revenue.

Even after a charity has been registered, the Inland Revenue can and will refuse tax relief if the income of the charity is not in fact applied for charitable purposes.

Difficulties in registration

If you are convinced of your group's charitable nature but the Charity Commission are not, then persevere. Your case may be in the hands of an overcautious officer. The Women's Research and Resources Centre for example were initially informed by the Charity Commission that they could not register if they were a women only collective. Their solicitor disagreed and in the end the Charity Commission accepted their argument.

You can ask for a meeting or your solicitor can argue your case if he or she is experienced in charity law. The Charity Commission will sometimes advise you how you could change the wording of your draft constitution to satisfy both them and the Inland Revenue. A good solicitor may be able to show that the Commission's argument has no foundation in law. You may, as a last resort, have to drop or alter some of your proposed purposes.

In your dealings with the Charity Commission it is most effective to remain polite and cautious. It is in your interests to be well briefed and you may need to be flexible. If you are convinced you have a good case, you and your solicitor may need to be insistent. Don't be beaten down by delays or mystification.

Appeals

If after corresponding with the executive of the Charity Commission over your draft governing instrument, you think their reluctance to register your organisation is legally wrong you can ask for a formal 'rehearing'. You can also request this if the Charity Commission have rejected your formal application for registration.

A rehearing is conducted by the three Commissioners sitting as a board. You will be asked to submit a written reasoned statement arguing your case. Since this will require detailed knowledge of charity law you will need to engage a knowledgeable solicitor, if you haven't already, to prepare it on your behalf. The rehearing is itself free, although you will have to pay your solicitor's fee.

If the outcome of the rehearing is not in your favour your next recourse is an appeal to the Chancery Division of the High Court, thence to the Court of Appeal and finally (with consent) to the House of Lords. Very few organisations appeal to the High Court for it is an expensive course of action, for which legal aid is not available and in respect of which (contrary to the normal rule) you cannot recover your costs from the Charity Commission or Inland Revenue if you win.

5 Legal formats

As soon as a group of individuals comes together to pursue a joint activity they will need to form an organisation. The courts will deem them to have a constitution even if it is not written down. It is therefore important to draw up a constitution for your organisation for three reasons:

- to define and agree the objects and powers of the group and the means of achieving them
- for the good and equitable conduct of your organisation and to avoid disputes at a later date
- to eventually obtain charitable status

The choices – unincorporated or incorporated

The major options are:

Unincorporated organisations

(a) Unincorporated association, society or club
(b) Trust
(c) Friendly Society

Incorporated organisations

(a) Company
(b) Industrial and Provident Society

The major legal difference between unincorporated and incorporated organisations is that an incorporated organisation has a corporate legal existence independent of the individuals that are its members. Thus while it is only able to act through its members, an incorporated organisation has rights and duties in its own right.

26

The implications of this are evident when one realises that since an unincorporated organisation has no separate legal existence, any property acquired for its purposes must be held on its behalf by trustees.

Unincorporated associations, societies and clubs

The principle disadvantage of the charity established as an unincorporated trust, club or association is the unlimited personal liability to which its trustees (or officers or committee members where there are no trustees) will be exposed. For they personally will enter into contracts on behalf of the charity, and if it is sued, their names will appear on the summons or writ, and they will have to pay any damages. Although normally they will be entitled to be reimbursed out of the assets of the charity, this will be of limited consolation if the charity simply does not have the wherewithal. Common examples of such risks would be in respect of rental payments and repair obligations under a tenancy, or in respect of a hire purchase contract entered into by them on behalf of the charity.

Other disadvantages compared with corporate charities are the tendency to over-loose and insufficiently regulated structures; the absence of external statutory authority to provide support and control; expense encountered in passing on the assets to new trustees; and the risks and difficulties of raising funds on loan. See also 'Community Organisation: Forms of Organisation' by Harry Rajak listed under Further Reading.

However, in certain simple situations, where for example one wants to set up an organisation for a limited, specific and probably local purpose, the unincorporated association may be adequate. It can be registered with the Charity Commission so long as its objects are exclusively charitable and fulfil the other tests of charity mentioned in this book. If you decide to use this format you should either use a model constitution which has stood the test of time or get some good advice.

Very few clubs are charitable for they are usually insufficiently outward looking and tend to exist primarily for the benefit of their members.

In the following paragraphs most attention will be paid to companies limited by guarantee and trusts as these are the two most popular formats for charities.

Trusts

Trusts have been used since time immemorial to establish formal relationships between three parties. The first (the donor) agrees with the second (the trustees) to put into their hands money or property (the trust property) to be used for the benefit of the third party (the beneficiaries). The trustees are therefore the nominal owners of the trust property but may not benefit from it and must ensure that it is used for the purposes (the trusts) set out in the trust deed.

Most private trusts are set up to benefit individuals – usually the family of the person establishing it. Charitable trusts, however, are fundamentally different in that they are established for a purpose which the law recognises as charitable.

The trust relationship, simple in concept, can also be simple to create – word of mouth being technically sufficient. However, the Charity Commissioners, not surprisingly, require written evidence of the existence and nature of the trust in order that they may determine whether it is charitable or not.

The advantages of the trust

Quick and cheap to set up

Quick and usually relatively cheap to set up, the trust is the traditional format for charities. The trust constitution, known as the Trust Deed, can be short if the trusts (purposes) are simple, and can be prepared without reference to any outside authority. As a result, no statutory fees or taxes are payable on formation of a trust. Accordingly, to save time and money at the outset, the trust is an easier format than the company. But it is not often that time and expense ought to take precedence over all other factors.

The trust can be cheap to run

There are few statutory requirements governing trusts, and thus the formalities and expense of running one are minimised. By and large they consist of such paperwork as the trustees consider fit and as the trust deed itself may stipulate. As to the duty to keep accounts, see page 44. Unlike companies, trusts are not required to present or prepare *audited* accounts. Since auditors fees are very rarely less than £100, unless the service is donated, this can represent a significant annual saving.

Trust constitutions can be easily amended

Provided that the trust deed was drafted to allow changes in its terms, the speed and ease of effecting such changes can be a significant advantage compared to the highly controlled, laborious and expensive procedure which is obligatory for companies. However, the Charity Commissioners are reluctant to accept for registration a trust which allows in its constitution for changes in its *charitable objects*, because this can cause problems in relation to gifts made for the original purposes only. Amendment to a trust deed must be by a document under seal, i.e. a deed.

Simplicity

Where the charity is of a non-participative kind, the trust format is likely to be sufficient in scope. It is particularly suitable for 'static charities', such as one to keep a named church in repair.

The position of trustees under a trust deed

Companies have a two-tier power structure so that although the directors hold day-to-day power, the ultimate power of removing the directors belongs to the members of the company. In contrast the trustees of a trust (who are equivalent in many ways to the directors of a company) normally have no check on themselves other than the limits of the trust deed and the law. Thus, if they regularly fail to use their powers effectively, or even at all, there is usually no means of unseating the trustees apart from removal, see page 44. Usually neither the commissioners nor the courts will comment upon the quality of the trustees' performance, but only its legitimacy according to the terms of the trust deed and the general law of trusts. (Trustees should, though, be aware of the extent of their financial liability described in chapter 6.) Depending, therefore, upon your own vantage point, this invulnerability to 'outside' interference may appear to you either as an advantage or as a disadvantage.

All trusts must have at least two trustees, but there is no maximum limit placed by law on the number of trustees. Most charitable trusts appear to have an odd number of trustees ranging from three to nine. An uneven number avoids deadlock voting. The trust deed should clearly specify the circumstances in which trustees can be forcibly removed and by whom. For further details on this point see page 44.

Friendly Societies

Friendly Societies were an invention of the last century when massive numbers of these self-help voluntary associations were set up to stave off the terrors of sickness, indigence and misfortune. Today they are of declining popularity and in 1977 only 38 new societies, mainly working mens' clubs, were formed, while over 150 were dissolved. It is not known how many of the 38 were charities – probably few, if any.

It is possible to be both a Friendly Society and a charity, in which case the society is exempt from registration with the Charity Commission but must register with the Registry of Friendly Societies under the Friendly Societies Act 1974, see Useful Organisations. The relatively simple structure, the ease of transferring property and the recourse to fairly cheap arbitration at the Registry's office in the case of disputes are advantages afforded by becoming a Friendly Society. While this may appeal to some small charitable groups, such as those concerned with mutual relief of hardship, most decide to go one step further and become incorporated as either a company or maybe as an Industrial and Provident Society.

Incorporated organisations

We have outlined the major difference, in terms of liabilities, between unincorporated and incorporated organisations on page 26. There are two forms of incorporated organisation – the Industrial and Provident Society and the limited company.

An incorporated organisation is a manufactured legal 'person'. It can sue and be sued, own property in its own name, die i.e. go into liquidation, change its character i.e. its constitution. It is owned by its members, who may be individuals and/or other incorporated organisations. It is operated by its committee or directors, who are elected and removable by the members.

What is a company?

There are two main forms of limited company. The most usual in the field of commercial activity is the company limited by shares. This is almost always an unsuitable format for a charity to adopt. The lesser known form of company and the appropriate form for a charity, is the company limited by guarantee.

In the company limited by shares, liability for the debts of

30

A manufactured legal person.

the company is limited to the face value of the paid-up shares held by the shareholders. Whereas, in a company limited by guarantee, there are no shareholders, but the members who must be at least two in number, agree to guarantee to pay any debts of the company up to a limit of normally £1 each. These members then elect the directors to run the company.

Almost anyone can be a member of a limited company, but usually membership is confined to those most closely associated with the charity, whether supporters or workers. The relationship between members and directors is complex. If you require specific advice or clarification, you should seek this from a specialist in the field.

Companies are now governed by the Companies Acts of 1948 onwards. Company constitutions consist of a Memorandum (containing objects) and Articles of Association (rules).

Rather than form your own company, you can usually obtain a company from law agents or solicitors.

31

The advantages of the company format

Protection from risk

The company format was developed in the last century as a convenient method whereby a disparate group of people could associate together for a common but specific purpose in a convenient, controlled way and with limited personal liability.

The limitation was crucial, otherwise, if the company collapsed, those involved would not only loose what they had put into it, but all their other assets as well. This is why the vast majority of companies must carry the word 'limited' after their name. If a charity, which is a company, wishes to drop the word 'limited' from its name, it must apply to the Department of Trade and Industry for permission under Section 19 of the Companies Act 1948. Permission will only be given on certain grounds and terms.

As we explain on page 38, the directors of a corporate charity are in broadly the same position as the trustees of a charitable trust in that both act as *trustees of the charity*. Directors of charitable companies are, therefore, subject to the provisions of the Companies Acts and also to many of the laws controlling trustees.

A ready-made constitution

The Companies Acts 1948-1967 provide a ready-made comprehensive constitution which tailored to the circumstances of the particular charity will sustain the day to day pressures and strains which will be placed on the constitution of any dynamic, participatory charity. For example a full mechanism is provided by the Companies Act 1948 Model Constitution (known as Table 'C') to control and regulate a 'fight' over who shall run the charitable company, i.e. be its directors. Table 'C' also includes detailed provisions for the holding of general and directors meetings; voting rights; altering members rights and the constitution of the company, and so on. The members can add to or subtract from Table 'C' as, within certain limits upon which a lawyer will advise, they think fit. Anyone can be a member if the directors admit them to membership within the constitution.

Democratic participation

The desire for the participation of those involved with or working for a charity militates strongly in favour of adopting a company format or becoming an Industrial and Provident Society. These forms of organisation have evolved over the last century as

32

the nearest thing we have to a democratic organisation within the State. They depend for their effectiveness on the involvement of their members.

Control of the directors

The members can oust or change their directors. There is no way in which the constitution of a company can lawfully be framed to defeat this right. To build a procedure for ousting into a trust deed is a complicated and expensive exercise, unless one is operating along a well-worn path where precedents exist.

Industrial and Provident Societies

The Registry of Friendly Societies has the statutory job of overseeing the life and times of Industrial and Provident Societies (IPSs) as well as that of Friendly Societies. Its two charges are somewhat different animals. Whereas the unincorporated Friendly Society is in effect a form of partnership of individuals, the IPS is an incorporated organisation with an identity distinct from its members.

An IPS will be charitable if it fulfills the normal criteria. Although it does not have to register with the Charity Commission, being exempt under the 1960 Act, if you plan to set up a charitable IPS, it is wise to send a draft set of rules to the Charity Division of the Inland Revenue to obtain their guidance on whether they would accept the IPS as charitable for tax purposes. This does not ensure that you will obtain tax relief when you apply, but it is the nearest you can come to gaining advance recognition.

Becoming a charitable IPS is an unusual and therefore somewhat untested procedure. Applicants, other than housing associations, may find it difficult to satisfy the two sets of requirements, those for being charitable and those for being an IPS.

An organisation qualifies for registration as an IPS if it is a society for carrying on an industry, business or trade and is *either* a bona fide co-operative society *or* is intended to be conducted for the benefit of the community. Only an IPS within the last mentioned category will be charitable.

Fortunately the Registry interprets the qualifications fairly liberally. But it is clear that to fall into the category of being *for the benefit of the community* the society must be non-profit-making and must be prohibited by its rules from distributing its assets among members. In common with an IPS registered under

33

the co-operative clause, control should be vested in the members equally and only moderate interest can be paid on share or loan capital. Other restrictions apply but they are unlikely to worry an organisation of charitable intent.

Broadly speaking the rules of any organisation registering under the 1965 Act have to comply with the list of requirements set out in the First Schedule to the Act, all of which are in any event matters which a prudent group of people would want to sort out in advance. More details are available in form F.617 available from the Registry of Friendly Societies.

The advantages and disadvantages of the IPS format

Those wanting to establish corporate charities may wish to compare the IPS format to the limited company format.

The rules and formalities of the IPS are less rigid, complex and onerous than are those for companies. This no doubt relates to the fact that IPSs are not primarily profit-generating organisations, whereas commercial companies are, and charitable companies are swept along with mainstream non-charitable companies when it comes to regulations.

An IPS can convert into a limited company if that ever proves to be necessary or desirable. And a company can likewise convert into an IPS.

Unless it consists of two or more registered societies an IPS requires at least seven members. A company only requires two members.

If an IPS registers using model rules submitted through a 'promoting society' such as the National Federation of Housing Associations it can be quite quick and cheap to register, for you are unlikely to need a solicitor and the Registry's special fee for applicants using model rules is £105. If you do not use model rules it is necessary to send your draft rules to the Registry for comment before finalising them. This procedure may well take about one year and the fee is £224. By comparison a company can be formed in a month or so although extra time must be added for registration with the Charity Commission, which takes from eight weeks to two years. The fee for registering a company is £50 plus the cost of printing, seal, statutory book etc (approx. £30) and any solicitors fees.

By setting up as a company and registering with the Charity Commission you can be fairly certain from the start that the Inland

34

Revenue and rating authority will treat your organisation as entitled to tax and rate relief. By contrast unless an IPS registers with the Registry of Friendly Societies using model rules which are accepted by the Inland Revenue as charitable, it will be necessary to demonstrate to the Inland Revenue that the IPS is charitable before it can obtain tax relief.

Summary

The unincorporated organisation, such as the trust, is the simpler, cheaper, but less protective vehicle for a charity. Whereas the incorporated format, such as the limited company, is more likely to be effective where either the charity's operations are complex and widespread or its employees or supporters need to be closely involved in the operation of the charity.

Whatever legal format you adopt, your organisation will require some form of constitution. We now outline the major elements in any constitution.

Your constitution

The constitution, or governing instrument, is to a charity as bricks are to a house. If it is wrongly put together, it can shackle the charity for evermore. It is, therefore, essential that unless you are following a model, which really does fit what you intend to do, you should get good advice from someone experienced in drawing up such documents.

These are some of the major matters which the constitution ought to cover:

Objects

The most important clause of any constitution is that which defines what the organisation is in existence to do i.e. its purposes. In drafting the objects, it is important not to define them too narrowly. In this way if circumstances change, or the organisation evolves, you will find that the proposed new activities are still within the original definition.

It is also important to resist the temptation to draw up your objects clause as a ringing statement of social commitment. This can lead to delays and difficulties. In a recent case an applicant first stated as part of their draft objects clause that they wished to promote the observation of the Sex Discrimination Act and that they were part of the Women's Movement.

This wording suggested campaigning and political activities, rather than advancing education. Fortunately the Charity Commission accepted that the organisation intended to fulfill charitable purposes in the legal sense and so together with the organisation's solicitor, they devised a suitable and unevangelical objects clause which nonetheless gave them the scope for all they wanted to do, as follows:

> The objects shall be to advance the education of women by carrying out and/or assisting the research and study into the social, economic and legal position of women in society, and to publish the results of such research and study.

Powers

The constitution should clearly define the powers (or means) by which the objects (or ends) can be obtained. A 'power' is a discretion, and need not be exercised. But as with objects, it usually pays to give your trustees/directors maximum room for action.

It is worth mentioning that if they are given wide powers, trustees/directors can themselves in effect make internal 'rules' or guidelines for the charity. They may, for example, specify standing orders for meetings, or rules about use of trust property. Such day to day arrangements are not suitable for inclusion in the constitution itself.

On the other hand, the trustees/directors may delegate the exercise of their powers, particularly those to draw up internal 'rules' or guidelines, if the constitution so allows. For further information see page 43.

Trustees/directors

It is the trustees of a trust, the directors of a company, and the committee of an unincorporated association who will have executive power to run the organisation. It is vital, therefore, that the scope of their authority is clearly defined. Usually the wider scope you can specify the better.

It is important to describe clearly the circumstances in which they can be removed and new appointments made. See page 41.

Members

As we explained earlier, most trusts do not have members as distinct from trustees. On the other hand, all companies do, as is the case with most unincorporated associations. It is sensible to define clearly what the rights and duties of membership are, and how new members can be made and existing ones removed. It is also prudent to stake out the constitutional relationship between members on the one hand and trustees or directors on the other.

Delegation

See page 41.

Altering the constitution

To provide against unforeseen future circumstances it is a good idea to give power for the constitution to be changed, though you will need to think carefully about the conditions which must be satisfied in the process. Other than in unusual circumstances (see page 7) it is best to entrench the objects clause, by making it unchangeable. This will avoid problems and conflict.

Elections

If you are to elect any of the officers then the mechanics need to be clearly spelt out. One of the advantages of the company is that full provisions are made in the Companies Acts, particularly in the model regulations known as Table C.

Investment

It is important to define the investment powers of the governing body of the charity, see pages 43 and 53.

Bank accounts

Opening and operating arrangements for bank accounts should also be provided for. It usually makes sense for the governing body to be able to instruct the bank to accept the signatures of whoever they may chose to operate the accounts of the organisation, even if the signatories are not themselves on the governing body.

Dissolution

Provisions for winding up the organisation need to be defined, see page 16.

We deal with most of these matters in greater detail in other parts of this text. It is worth saying, however, that the time spent in careful preparation of the constitution of a prospective charity will be time well spent. To leave things to be sorted out as they arise can well be a recipe for unresolved conflict.

6 Charity trustees and the running of a charity

Charity trustees

The term 'trustee' can be confusing. All charities must have charity trustees. The term is defined as 'the persons having the general control and management of the charity'. In a charitable trust they are the people appointed as trustees in the trust deed but in a company established for charitable purposes, the directors are the equivalent of the charity trustees. In this chapter we use the term 'trustee' to cover all forms of charity trustee.

Charity law governs the actions of these people in so far as they are trustees of a charity and it is primarily this role that we will consider in this chapter. At the same time we must make it clear that the trustee-directors of a charitable company are subject to company law as well.

Choosing the right trustees for a charity is crucial. It can also be a bit baffling. Should you invite friends, or eminent names or local worthies? What qualities or abilities will the trustees need? Can they be paid? What responsibilities are they taking on?

Responsibilities of trustees

In a nutshell, the trustees of a charity have full control of what the charity does and how it does it. Their first duty is to ensure that the purposes, or objects, of the charity are properly carried out as laid down in the constitution of the charity. This means, for example, that they are required to ensure the funds and assets of the charity are properly administered and used. The Charity Commission issues two free booklets entitled *Responsibilities of Charity Trustees* and *The Charity Commissioners: how they can help Charity Trustees* which set out the bones of this topic.

Choosing trustees

As with anything else, you will want to balance your trustees and the skills or advantages which each of them will bring to the task. The right balance will be determined by the nature and level of activity planned for the charity. Bear in mind that the trustees collectively have the final say on all matters affecting the life of a charity. So you should choose trustees who are broadly in sympathy with what you are trying to do, as well as personally compatible. Generally speaking it is more important that they are likely to prove committed and capable than that they be eminent. Obviously, and in all cases, they need to be absolutely trustworthy.

The trustees must ensure the charity's purposes are carried out.

The Charity Commission are not usually concerned with the identity of proposed trustees in any direct way. However, the Commission will be comforted by the knowledge that the proposed trustees are people who have a reputation to lose and who, by being willing to act as trustees, show their own confidence in the applicant charity. This consideration can be particularly helpful where the organisation seeking registration is unconventional in its aims.

You should also bear in mind the importance to fund-raising of having well-known people openly associated with your charity. But since they are, by definition, likely to have many other calls on their time, one can sometimes get the best of both worlds by engaging these 'big names' as patrons rather than trustees. The title 'patron' is a purely honorary one, which does not give them either the power or the responsibility which attaches to a trustee. In this way people can lend their name and backing to your cause without becoming embroiled in the running of the organisation.

Paying trustees and worker-trustees

The Charity Commission take the view that generally the trustees of a charity should not make a profit out of their position, nor should they be placed in a position where their duties and responsibilities as trustees might conflict with their own interests. Accordingly, the Commission will generally refuse to register an applicant whose constitution does not prohibit payment to trustees, though there are broad exceptions.

The first is in respect of professional trustees, such as solicitors and accountants, where the Commission will allow the constitution to provide for their remuneration in the normal way. It is therefore wise to include the following clause in your constitution:–

> Any trustee for the time being hereof being a solicitor or other person engaged in any profession shall be entitled to charge and be paid all usual professional or other charges for work done by him or his firm in connexion with the execution of the trusts hereof.

Where a charity wishes to involve its employees in directing the affairs of the charity through the appointment of worker-trustees, it is likely to meet problems. The Charity Commission used to permit the appointment of paid workers of the charity to trusteeship, provided the trustee brought special skills to the administration of the charity and so long as safeguards were built in to prevent the trustee benefiting from the office. The standard safeguards were that the number of remunerated trustees be less than a majority of the quorum and that any such trustees be absent from meetings that consider their own appointment, conditions of service or pay.

While these safeguards are still those insisted on by the Charity Commissioners, they are currently very reluctant to permit even this much worker control. In very exceptional cases they may agree to register a charity with provision for such appointments but only when a particular trustee has "special qualifications which are not otherwise available to the charity and which would make for its more effective administration" and only when such "provisions are necessary and reasonable in the exceptional circumstances."

If you require more worker control than this, you can consider establishing a charitable company of which the charity workers are the only members and are thus in the position to hire and fire the trustee-directors. Alternatively you could register as an Industrial and Provident Society for the benefit of the community with charity workers making up part or all of the membership of the society. In the latter case your access to charitable benefits will be at the discretion of the Revenue. Both alternatives are problematic and assistance should be sought from an advisor knowledgeable in this field.

Whether or not one seeks to have employee-trustees, it is normal and acceptable to provide in the constitution that the trustees can be paid their out-of-pocket expenses incurred in connection with acting as trustees, as well as arrangements for payment of reasonable interest on monies lent to the trust or property let to it.

Delegation of trustees' powers

The normal rule is that trustees cannot delegate their powers unless the constitution of the charity expressly allows. Especially where the charity is likely to be an active and busy one it makes sense to provide in the constitution for delegation. This will mean that whether or not you have a limited power of appointment of worker-trustees, you can involve employees on any committees. If this is desired regulation 52 of Table C of the Companies Act 1948 will need to be extended in the Articles of a charitable company.

The Charity Commission will insist that all delegated powers can be withdrawn (revoked) by the trustees at any time. It is also as well to stipulate that any committee with delegated powers must promptly inform the trustees of their decisions and activities.

A busy charity may well want to operate its bank account on the signature of some, or even none, of its trustees. This power should be spelt out very clearly in the constitution for the benefit of the bank.

Liability of trustees/directors

Where a charity trustee acts fraudulently (deceitfully) nothing will protect him or her against personal liability without limit to whoever incurs loss as a result. This is equally true for the directors of a charitable company as it is for the trustees of a charitable trust.

Where it is a question of negligence or of acting outside the limits of the trust (that is to say, beyond the scope of the objects or as the law puts it, ultra vires) the trustee's liability to the public on the one hand and the beneficiaries on the other may be different.

Broadly speaking the trustees of a charitable trust and the directors of a charitable company are liable personally without limit to compensate the charity if they allow the monies to be spent for purposes not sanctioned by the constitution, or if they lose the charity money by dealing with its funds or assets in a way which is not authorised by its constitution or under the general law of charities.

As regards outsiders (third parties), the trustees of a trust or committee of an unincorporated association are personally liable without limit, although normally they can recover what they have to pay out insofar as the charity has sufficient assets to reimburse them. (The committee of an unincorporated association can only make the general members of the association personally liable if the constitution clearly gives them that power or if the members sanction the liability within the constitution.) However, the directors of a charitable company are in this respect at a real advantage, in that they will not be personally liable. Any claim is against the company as such, and its liability is limited to the extent of its assets. That said most charity trustees would probably not wish to see innocent creditors bear the cost of a charitable company's insolvency. In any event a charity should only undertake obligations that it can meet and should not act speculatively.

If charity trustees or other persons controlling a charity are worried about whether a proposed course of action on behalf of the charity is proper, they had better seek advice from a solicitor or the Charity Commission. The advice of the latter is likely to be very conservative and by requesting it questions may be raised in the mind of the Charity Commission which need never have occurred.

However, advice given by the Commission in knowledge of the full facts, serves as some protection for the charity trustees who act on it, because their action cannot then be regarded as a breach of trust. If you require this protective advice, you must write to the Charity Commissioners with the full facts and ask for their opinion under section 24 of the Charities Act.

The powers of trustees

Trustees have certain statutory powers (and limitations) such as under the Trustee Acts and Trustee Investments Acts. In addition they will have the further powers (and limitations) set out in the constitution of the charity. See page 36.

Some statutory obligations cannot be overridden by a constitution. Within this limitation one golden rule of setting up a charity is to give its trustees and therefore the charity the widest discretions. For example, and always assuming that you can find trustees in whom you have confidence, you should provide the widest discretion as to how the trustees can invest the charity's assets; as to whom and on what terms it can lend charity funds and borrow funds; as to how the charity is managed; as to if and when to dissolve (i.e. wind-up) the charity and then to decide as to which other charity or charitable purpose to pass any surplus.

Limitations on trustees' power

Certain obligations and restrictions are placed on trustees by the law, which the constitution of the charity cannot always override. For example:

(a) They must notify the Charity Commission of any changes in the registered particulars of their charity such as any change in its constitution.

(b) If for any reason the purposes of the charity cannot be carried into practical effect within the terms of the governing instrument they must apply to the Charity Commission for directions or for what is known as a scheme to change the trusts.

(c) Before a charity can sell land or buildings or lease them for more than 21 years, the trustees must usually obtain an order of the Charity Commission.

(d) If the constitution does not so provide, borrowing by the charity, even a bank overdraft, is not permitted without the consent of the Charity Commission. If you are in doubt contact the Charity Commission.

(e) The trustees are required to obtain skilled advice on investing the charity's money and are also required to review the investments from time to time. See Charities Official Investment Fund under Useful Organisations, and *Investment Management by Charity Trustees* under Further Reading.

43

Reappointment and replacement of trustees

The usual system is that trustees of a charitable trust hold office until and unless they retire or are removed. In a trust set up by an individual it is not unusual to provide that the power of appointment is exercisable by the founder. Where nothing is provided, the Trustee Acts give power of appointment to the continuing trustees. In the case of corporate charities Table C of the Companies Act is often followed, which provides for automatic retirement of trustee-directors after a number of years.

In any event your constitution should specify who has the power to appoint and remove trustees. If it is a corporate charity these powers must reside in the members, who can number employees and potential beneficiaries in their ranks.

The Charity Commissioners have the power to discharge trustees and officers of a charity in cases of misconduct or mis-management. They may also remove a charity trustee where he or she has been convicted of felony (a grave crime), or is bankrupt, or is incapable of acting by reason of mental disorder or when a trustee's failure to act impedes the proper administration of the charity.

Charity accounts

Charity trustees have a general duty to ensure that the charity keeps normal and proper accounts, usually consisting of an income and expenditure account and a balance sheet as at the end of the account period. Almost all new charities are required to send their annual statement of account to the Charity Commission each year. These are open to public inspection. In any case the books of account and statements of account must be preserved by the charity for at least seven years.

You can present your accounts in almost any standard form but you may find it useful to obtain the forms produced by the Charity Commission.

Charities are not required to have their accounts audited unless they are charitable companies or IPSs which are required by law to present annual audited accounts and returns to Companies House and the Registry of Friendly Societies respectively. Since the audit must be conducted under the direction of a certified or chartered accountant this will usually prove to be expensive, unless you can obtain concessionary help from sympathetic accountants.

Whether or not you have to have your accounts audited it is most important to institute a useful bookkeeping system from the time of the foundation of a charity. Small charities can use very simple systems but if you fail to set one up early enough or fail to operate it accurately, you will store up time-consuming problems for yourselves and will not be able to institute an effective system of financial control and management. Furthermore without evidence of proper financial systems you will find it difficult to obtain funding.

Charity stationery

No regulations govern what has to be shown on the notepaper and documents of a charity *as such* but we recommend you include a small line such as 'A registered charity, number xxx.'

If the charity is a company or IPS then the word 'limited' must appear as the last word of the name unless a special statutory declaration is filed at companies house or unless you obtain permission from the Registry of Friendly Societies. In which case your stationery must still state that the charity is a limited company or IPS.

The stationery of companies should also state the place of registration of the company, its registered number and the address of its registered office. If you name the directors, you must name them all and give the nationality of any that are not nationals of EEC countries.

7 Charities, politics and campaigning

Charities are not permitted to have directly political objects. They are therefore restricted in the nature of the campaigning work they can undertake. But many charities are overcautious.

The law allows a degree of political activity by charities if it is in pursuit of their objects. As the Charity Commissioners put it in their Report for 1976, '. . . a charity is not prohibited from engaging in political activities provided that these are carried out in furtherance of its objects'.

But it is clear that a body which has as an object to change the law in some way, will not be registered as a charity. Further, regardless of its objects, if the main weight of a charity's activity is directed to changing the law it is acting outside charitable limits.

Permissible political activity

Some political activity directly ancillary to or in furtherance of the charitable objects of a charity is permissible such as to:

(a)   provide information and advice when this is requested by government officials

(b)   comment on green or white papers

(c)   provide members of either House of Parliament with arguments for or against a published bill and give continuous advice on the implications of the bill and any amendments

(d)   in some other cases, not involving legislation, a charity is entitled to persuade a Member to support its cause in Parliament. For instance, where the question arises whether a government grant is to be made or continued to a particular charity

(e) non-political parliamentary activity as for example supporting enabling legislation granting a charity wider powers to carry out its purposes.

(f) presenting reasoned memos to MPs

If the political activities you envisage fall outside these categories, they may still be permissible if they are directly ancillary to the main objects of your charity and do not absorb a substantial part of your charity's cash or other resources. For example, it is probably lawful for an information campaign to be organised and financed by a disaster relief charity to get the government to intervene with taxpayers money in some overseas tragedy. It is fair

Charities are not permitted to have directly political objects.

to point out though that this is sensitive territory for the Charity Commission who are unhappy about this type of activity. Similarly, for a housing charity to canvas for greater allocation of national resources for housing, or for the enactment of greater legal safeguards for tenants, would not of itself put that organisation beyond the charitable pale.

Sanctions and clarification

If a charity is found to have engaged in impermissible political activities the trustees may be asked to pay to the charity the funds which have been misapplied. The charity will almost certainly forfeit to the Inland Revenue the tax relief on the misapplied funds. But the charity would not lose its charitable status, provided it dropped its unlawful activities.

It is unfortunate that the House of Lords, the highest court in the land, has not lately had the opportunity of redefining and clarifying the limits of charitable activity. The extension of statute law into every corner of our day to day lives makes it impossible for the socially concerned charity to operate 'beyond' politics and statutory considerations.

Parallel political organisations

Several charities, realising that some of their proposed activities would fall the wrong side of the dividing line between what is and what is not permitted by way of political activity, have established separate non-charitable organisations to carry on the forbidden functions. On other occasions a non-charitable organisation has hived off its charitable activities. The Cobden Trust with its political and campaigning arm the National Council for Civil Liberties, and Public Interest Research Centre with Social Audit are cases in point.

The Charity Commissioners are sometimes uneasy at this way of resolving the political dilemma, since the theoretical separation of the two sympathetic organisations may in practice degenerate into a single administration. Given the severe manpower limitations which afflicts their watchdog role, the Commissioners have tended to discourage this structure at application stage. In practice it is therefore advisable to take professional advice and prepare the ground thoroughly concerning the practicalities of separating the two bodies, so that the Commission can be reassured that the mechanics of cost apportionment and cross-accounting between the two bodies have been confronted and properly resolved.

General considerations

In practice the Charity Commission are fairly reluctant to confront established charities over any quasi-political activities which they undertake. This sensitive area of charity practice is one in which a good deal of tact and restraint has avoided, thus far, too many collisions.

For further information you should consult the *Reports of the Charity Commissioners*, especially that for 1969, which provide some limited guidance. See also 'Campaigning and Charitable Status' in Further Reading.

Educational campaigns and propaganda

The distinction between public education, which is permitted to charities, and propaganda, which isn't, is also very fine. A vigorous campaign run by a charity to inform the public of the needs of its beneficiaries is acceptable so long as people are *informed*.

What isn't acceptable is when a charity's campaign is only advancing its own preferred solution to a problem. This is then straying into becoming propaganda rather than being public education. In 1978 an established charity was advised by the Charity Commissioners that an article in its magazine was political propaganda and therefore not a proper charitable activity, as it was 'provocative and one-sided'.

8 Charities and money earning

Charging for goods and services

One of the key questions in budgeting for a charity is whether or not one can charge for the goods or services made or rendered by that charity. Here we are not considering goods or services in the nature of trade, but benefits which a charity bestows on people as part of its charitable activities.

One only has to realise that virtually all private schools and private hospitals are registered charities to realise not only that a charity may charge for services rendered but that it can be a very considerable charge if those services warrant it.

Here we must introduce a word of warning against making charges so high that the charity endangers its status by ceasing to benefit a sufficient section of the public (see page 15). Youth clubs, museums and sports centres, to name a few diverse types of charity, commonly make charges in one way or another. In each of these cases, however, the charges will only represent a part of the cost of providing the services concerned. The question then arises as to whether or not a charity can make a 'profit' from, for example, the publication of its research.

Profit

Invariably a charity will find that even though there may be an *apparent* profit on a charge or sale, if it adds in the real costs of providing it – in our example the aggregate costs of the research leading to the publications – it is not making a true net profit.

In rare cases, however, a charity may find that it makes a true net profit from its charitable activities at the end of the year. There are two potential dangers in this situation. The first is that doubt may be cast upon the 'public benefit' of what the charity is doing. That is to say, a commercial organisation might be able to do a similar job at a similar price if it follows a similar course and pricing policy. The second potential danger is that the charity will be close to wandering over the hazy line between pursuing its charitable objects (and raising revenue in the process but as a secondary consequence) and trading as a primary purpose.

The Inland Revenue might, where a net profit was made over the year, try to interpret it as a trading profit on which Corporation Tax should be levied and it might be very difficult to pursuade a court otherwise. The safe course, therefore, is to ensure that no net surplus results overall in respect of the true expenditure and income account for those activities (leaving out of account, for example, donations).

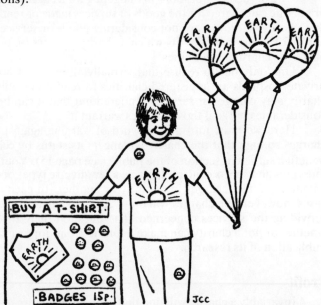

The begging bowl approach is giving way to trading of one kind or another.

51

Benefits to the donor

A danger to avoid is the tax rule that states that someone who makes a covenant to a charity with the intention that the charity will be able to recover tax at the standard rate from the Inland Revenue, see page 58, will not be treated as having made a charitable covenant if he or she receives benefits in exchange. So, for example, a museum which gives members certain benefits such as reduced entry fees in exchange for annual subscriptions cannot strictly speaking relieve a member from the obligation of paying annual subscriptions simply because he or she has made a covenant of greater annual value than the subscription each year. In practice the Inland Revenue may well not take a rigid line and seek to disallow such arrangements. But it would not be wise to rely on this.

Occasional fund-raising

Normally, fund-raising which involves charging people, and which is carried on on a regular basis, stands the risk of being treated as a taxable 'trade' by the Inland Revenue and taxed accordingly, at corporation tax rates. However, by concession the Revenue will not seek to tax the funds raised so long as the following conditions are satisfied:

(1) The organisation is not regularly trading;
(2) The trading is not in competition with other traders;
(3) The activities are supported substantially because the public are aware that any profits will be devoted to charity;
(4) The profits are transferred to charities or otherwise applied for charitable purposes.

Inland Revenue leaflet C5.

Can charities trade?

Trade as such is not a charitable object even though it provides the funds for a charity to do its work. Although trading cannot of itself be a charitable *object* it is prudent to give a charity the *power* to trade from the outset. So long as the trade is modest in amount (occasional fund-raising activities) there is little danger of the balance of activities getting out of gear through the trade ceasing to be merely ancillary and becoming a mainstream activity (see page 15).

In two cases, however, trade may be allowable by charity law, and exempt under tax law. The first is where the trade is a direct and necessary implementation of the very object of the charity.

The second is where the trade activity is mainly carried out by the beneficiaries of the charity, as well as implementing its objects. Only in a few rare instances does this happy coincidence occur, for example workshops for the blind which produce goods for sale in the course of the rehabilitation of those for whom the charity exists.

Charities increasingly rely on self-help to keep themselves going. The begging bowl appears to be giving way to trading activities of one kind or another, such as mail-order selling, charity shops, retailing third world products and the sale of Christmas cards. As we explain on page 50 it has long been traditional for certain types of charity to charge for the services rendered in the course of carrying out their charitable purposes (schools and hospitals in particular). But substantial trading simply and solely to generate funds which are then spent in pursuit of the charitable objects is a growing practise. How is it done within the law?

How is it done?

The common method now used to engage in substantial trade is for a separate trading organisation, usually a company with share capital and limited liability, to be established for the charity. This company is not subject to the laws of charity, and so is free to trade more or less like any commercial company. So long as the trading company covenants (i.e. commits in writing) its profits (both revenue and capital profits) for a period exceeding three years back to the charity, the net result is broadly the same in terms of tax advantages as if the charity had been allowed to carry out the trade itself. In short, no corporation tax will be paid and all the profits can be passed to the charity.

If the trading company retains some of the profit, it will be subject to corporation tax. It may be necessary to take professional advice on this.

Under this scheme the trading company has to pay basic rate income tax on the covenanted money and it can take up to a year for the charity to recover this from the Revenue. To avoid this delay you can use Section 256 of the 1970 Taxes Act if, and only if, the charity is also a limited company. Section 256 basically provides that when one company receives from another company any payments which are for corporation tax purposes charges on income and the company making the payment is a 51% subsidiary of the other, then the two companies may make a joint election that the payments may be made without deduction of income tax.

53

Trading through a separate limited company in this way has the advantage that it will insulate the funds of the charity against the risks of something going wrong with the trade, because the liability of the trading company is limited by law to the extent of its own assets.

Can the charity finance its trading company?

Strictly speaking the charity can only use its funds to pursue its objects or, meanwhile, to invest as its constitution allows. If a charity wants to establish a wholly-owned trading company, on the

```
THIS COVENANT is made the      day of         19
BETWEEN
           TRADERS              LTD. (hereinafter called
"the Company") of the one part and THE TRUSTEES OF
THE CHARITY CALLED "BOUNTIFUL"  (Registered
No. 257601) whose names are                    of
of            of            of                    and
of (hereinafter called "the Trustees") which
expression where the context admits includes the
survivors or last survivor of them and other the
Trustees or Trustee for the time being of the said
Charity of the other part.


WHEREAS the said Charity is a trust established for
charitable purposes only and the Company which exists
mainly for the purpose of carrying on trade
           has decided to make a covenanted donation
to charity within the meaning of Section 248 of the
Income and Corporation Taxes Act 1970 and to execute
this Covenant and carry into effect its obligations
accordingly

NOW THIS DEED WITNESSETH  as follows:

1.  IN each accounting period for the purposes of
    corporation tax the Company shall pay to the
    Trustees in accordance with the provisions of
    this Deed an annual sum equal to the profits
    of the Company for that period the same to be
    paid less income tax.

2.  THE Covenant hereinbefore contained shall
    commence within and include the accounting
    period during which this Deed is executed and
    shall continue until and include the accounting
    period ending on or after the 31st day of
    December 19    (Note: date to be at least
    4 years after the date of the Deed so as to
    obligate the company to make at least four
    annual payments.)
```

3. THE profits of the Company shall be its
    distributable profits as defined in paragraph
    10 of the Sixteenth Schedule to the Finance
    Act 1972 but without deducting

    (i)   the amount of the Corporation Tax which
          but for the said Section 248 would be
          payable in respect thereof or

    (ii) the annual sum payable under this
          Covenant

4. PAYMENTS hereunder shall be made annually in
    such manner and at such times as the Auditor
    for the time being of the Company shall in
    writing direct and subject thereto the Company
    shall at least two calendar months before the
    end of each accounting period pay (less income
    tax) a sum equal to the profits of the
    Company of that period as then estimated and
    in the event of any overpayment the excess
    shall be refunded at or after the end of the
    said period and in the event of any
    underpayment the shortfall shall be made good
    (less income tax) before the end of the said
    period *

5. NO payment hereunder shall be charged to
    capital and all payments hereunder shall be
    applied by the Trustees for the purposes of the
    said Charity

    IN WITNESS whereof the Common Seal of the
    Company has been hereunto affixed in the presence of
    two duly authorised officers of the Company the day
    and year first before written

    The COMMON SEAL of TRADERS LIMITED)
    was hereunto affixed in the presence of:)

        Director: Director/Secretary:

*   S.248(1) of the Taxes Act 1970 only allows such covenanted
    payments to be a pre-tax charge on profits if they are
    "paid in the accounting period" concerned. Thus the
    paying company will have to estimate its profits so
    as to enable that condition to be met. It is obviously
    better to overpay and obtain a refund when final accounts
    show the actual profit, and the wording of the covenant
    allows for this.

*Deed of covenant suitable for use by a trading company
set up to raise money for a charity.*

above lines, the promoters of the charity should make sure that from the outset its constitution allows the trustees to invest in the shares of a private company.

Similarly, if the trading company is going to need loan facilities, the constitution of the charity should make it clear from the outset that the trustees are free to make loans without security to any company in which the charity holds shares.

If any problem is experienced in gaining acceptance by the Charity Commission for such lending powers, at least the power to invest in shares in a private company should be included in your constitution. This is a relatively common and unobjectionable investment discretion for trustees to have. It will at least allow them to put money into the trading company by purchase of redeemable preference shares. This both provides the company with the funds to start up and will allow those funds to be repaid (i.e. the shares redeemed) when the trading is generating sufficient surplus funds.

Separating the charity and the trading company

If a charity sets up a separate trading company on the lines mentioned above, it is vital that the activities of the two are kept separate. Otherwise the charitable status of the charity could be put into jeopardy, since if there is a mingling of the funds of the two organisations it is probable that the charity will in the process cease to be exclusively charitable. What is more, since the charity generally cannot trade as a principal objective, it will be in breach of its constitution for its funds to be used to subsidise the trading company. It is therefore essential right from the start to keep separate accounts for the charity and the trading company.

Secondly, insofar as the two organisations share premises and facilities and insofar as personnel of the charity may from time to time spend some of their working hours on the business of the trading company, the expenses, rents and wages involved should be fairly divided between the charity and the trading company. In this way no hidden subsidy of the trading company takes place at the expense of the charity.

One simple way of doing this is to keep time sheets if one of the charity's employees spends normal working hours on trading company business. The rate to be charged should, of course, take account of overheads and national insurance as well as the actual salary of the charity employee concerned.

56

As regards shared premises, the total costs of the premises including rates, insurance, service charge and expenditures on repairs and decorations, should be calculated on a square footage basis, leaving the common parts such as corridors and toilets out of account, and apportioned between the charity and the trading company according to the area that they actually occupy.

Insofar as the trading company builds up a debt to the charity in the course of the year, it is sensible to discharge this amount on a regular basis, say every quarter. Otherwise another form of subsidy can creep into the arrangement in the form of hidden extended credit given by the charity to the trading company.

9 Charities and tax relief

This chapter is divided into two main sections. The first is concerned with taxes payable by donors; the second with taxes payable by recipient charities.

Taxes payable by donors

Four Year Covenants – Income Tax

Where an individual promises (i.e. covenants) to give to charity a sum of money out of his or her taxable income for more than three consecutive years (subject to intervening death) and that promise is made by Deed (that is to say formally, under Seal) then the charity which would benefit from this promise is by law entitled to recover income tax at basic rate on the amount of the annual donation. The effect of the covenant is that income tax at the basic rate (currently 30%) is diverted from the State to the charity so that the donor can properly consider that the true amount of the gift is not the net amount, but that amount together with basic rate tax calculated upon it.

In addition, since the budget of 1980, the donor, if he is a higher rate tax payer, will escape tax at the higher rate and where appropriate, investment income surcharge, on covenanted donations up to £3,000 gross per annum. It is therefore advisable to make it clear to covenantors that if they are higher rate tax payers they can afford to enter into a larger covenant than they might otherwise have done, because they will also be benefiting from the tax relief on their covenanted donations.

NB1 Where the donor receives any benefit from his or her covenant the tax privilege is lost. Several charities offend this rule without in fact losing their tax benefits, but Revenue generosity by inactivity cannot be relied upon.

NB2 Donors who do not pay tax at the basic rate on income equal to the amount of the gift are in a different position.

Four Year Covenants – Corporation Tax

Where a limited company makes a covenant similar to that of the individual (i.e. for over three years and by Deed) the 1970 Taxes Act allows it to make those payments out of its profits before corporation tax. That is to say the donations will be a charge on income and deductible by the company in computing its liability to corporation tax. Since that tax is now running at 52% for larger companies, this effectively enables a company to double up on its gifts (assuming that it makes taxable profits!)

NB1 As a matter of mechanics the company is required to deduct tax at basic income tax rate and hand it over to the Inland Revenue from whom the charity can claim a refund.

Forms of Covenant

Whether the 4-year covenant is made by an individual or a company the only requirement is that the amount to be paid to the charity year by year shall be ascertainable according to a formula established at the outset. Usually the covenant is for a fixed amount. But it is possible for a company, for example, to covenant a certain percentage of its profits, and so long as 'profits' is defined with certainty this will be a lawful covenant within the tax concession and will also have the advantage of relieving the company from making payments in the years when it has no profits, which would not be the case with the fixed sum covenant.

It is generally best to frame such a profits formula by reference to taxable profits before capital allowances. This should minimise fluctuations.

An individual trading alone or in partnership (partners are taxed individually) can make a similar covenant.

In order to recover income tax and corporation tax on covenanted donations, the charity should apply to the Inland Revenue Claims Branch, Charity Division. Many charities use the services of the Charities Aid Foundation to administer their covenanted income (see Useful Organisations).

Loan covenants

If a donor prefers to make a lump sum donation, it is still possible to execute this by covenant and obtain the tax advantage. In this case $\frac{1}{4}$ of the lump sum is deemed the first instalment of a four year covenant and the rest of the sum is an interest free loan to the

<u>Deed of Covenant</u>

I...

of..

....

HEREBY COVENANT with (registered name of

charity) (hereinafter called the 'Charity')

that for a period of four years from the

........day of...............19............

or during my life (whichever period be the

shorter). I will pay annually/quarterly/

monthly to the Charity out of my taxable

income £..................................

(sum in words)...............................

Signed sealed and delivered by me this.......

day of........................... 19.......

In the presence of..........................

....

Suitable form of covenant to be used by individuals covenanting to a charity.
Note that (a) the covenant payments can only be dated to start on or after the date of signing the deed (b) all deletion should be initialed (c) the witness must not be the spouse of the donor.

charity. Each of the subsequent three years another ¼ of the sum is deemed repaid by the charity to the donor, but is effectively given back by the donor to the charity as the next instalment of the covenant. To affect this no actual repayments have to be made by the charity but it has to reclaim the basic rate tax from the Revenue for each of the four years.

Tax-free gifts

Although covenanting is the most effective method of giving for a business to deploy, certain other limited payments count as business expenses and are therefore deductible for calculating tax. In outline these are donations for technical education conducted at approved institutes; approved research; and under Extra-Statutory Concession B7 through the local Inspector of Taxes, smallish gifts to local charities. In each case the education, research or projects must be related to the trade of the business. For further details consult *Charitable Giving and Taxation* listed under Further Reading.

Capital Transfer Tax (CTT)

This tax is payable on the value of all gifts, unless an exemption applies. The rate of tax is calculated on an upward sliding scale, the gifts which a person makes in his or her lifetime being totted up along the way. Without going into details of the tax, a charity will need to know the following:

(a) Up to one year before death, a benefactor can make gifts to charity without paying CTT. There is no limit to this exemption.

(b) Gifts totalling up to £250,000 made on death and in the year preceding death are also exempt from CTT.

(c) Gifts by one spouse to another are entirely exempt from CTT, so that if the exemptions of one spouse have been exhausted it may still be possible for monies or assets to be given by that spouse to the other and for him or her to give on to charity within the second spouse's exempt limit. But if there is a pre-existing agreement to do this, the gift by the second spouse will be treated as the gift of the first. Professional advice should be sought before relying on this opportunity.

(d) Where applicable, the CTT itself can be paid either by the recipient charity (although still with reference to the rate of tax of the donor) or by the donor. If the latter is the case, the CTT he or she pays will be treated as an addition to the gift on which it is levied, giving rise to further CTT liability (aptly known as 'grossing up'). This principle does not operate where the gift is made on death i.e. under the terms of a will.

Capital Gains Tax (CGT)

If a taxpayer makes a gift by transferring an asset to a charity then no capital gains tax (presently 30% of the chargeable gain) is payable. If, for example, someone owns shares on which he or she will realise a big taxable gain if they are sold, it avoids CGT if the actual shares are given to the charity. This leaves the charity free, if it would rather have cash, to sell the shares. In this way no CGT is payable.

Where the capital gain accruing to a charity is not applied for charitable purposes, then the Inland Revenue can cancel the CGT advantage to the extent of non-application.

Development Land Tax

This tax is chargeable where the development value of land is realised, for example, on sale or the commencement of a development project. A *gift* is not realisation for this purpose and charities are themselves exempt from paying this tax.

Wealth Tax

In the 1974 Green Paper foreshadowing wealth tax, it is expressly stated that charities would be exempt.

Non-residence

Where a donor is not domiciled in the UK for tax purposes and makes a gift of property which at the time of the gift is outside the UK, no CTT will be payable. Equally, such a person who makes payments to a UK charity under covenant will probably have to funnel that gift through a co-operative intermediate charity in their country of residence if they are to obtain whatever tax concessions there are available for charitable donations. The USA, for example, has much greater concessions than the UK. In this, as in so many other matters concerning tax, professional guidance is likely to be essential.

Halfway-house charities

Individuals or companies can often be encouraged to give more to charity if they set up their own 'halfway-house charity'. As we have already remarked one of the most pleasurable motives for many individuals and companies in giving to charity is the thought that hard earned income is to be diverted from the Inland Revenue to a charity of one's choice! But this can only happen if one is willing to commit oneself to giving to one particular charity for more than three years. Few people, or companies, want to be so single minded but would much rather spread their money around from year to year as they think it can be best utilised. The halfway-house charity provides a solution.

The key is to set up a simple charitable trust whose objects include all the four charitable heads. In short any money received by the charity can then be spent by the trustees on any charitable purpose.

The constitution of the trust should be short and simple, and to provide maximum scope should give the trustees the fullest discretion as regards power of investment and decision making. Here another advantage accrues. Without a halfway-house charity one can only make tax exempt covenants to an 'established' charity. With the halfway-house charity however, the trustees can give 'for charitable purposes'. This would allow them, for example, to make a grant to a non-charity or an individual so long as it was clearly earmarked and spent by that non-charity or individual for a charitable project or purposes. ('Established' in this sense tends in practice to be taken by the Inland Revenue to mean formally registered charities, although they should accept an unregistered charitable trust which is formally established and has some degree of permanence.)

Another advantage of the halfway house charity is that the person setting it up can be a trustee along with his 'nearest and dearest', although the Charity Commission like at least one trustee from outside the immediate family of the founder. Where a company sets up a charity however, it is usually perfectly satisfactory to confine one's trustees to directors and/or shareholders and/or employees.

Having established one's halfway-house charity the founder, be it company or individual, executes a conventional four year covenant in favour of the new halfway-house charity. Each year the trustees of this charity recover the tax exempted by the covenant and decide with full flexibility how to dole out this charitable money.

For a company that wishes to give to charity, a half-way house charity can have a further advantage. If several directors each has a different 'pet' good cause, or indeed no cause at all, joint agreement is more easily obtained to commit a sizeable sum to charity if flexibility can be built into the arrangements.

Taxes payable by charities

Income Tax and Corporation Tax

Under section 360 of the Income and Corporation Taxes Act 1970 the income of charities is exempt from income tax and corporation tax so long as it is applied for charitable purposes. In chapter 8 we have detailed the regulations governing income raised from trading by charities, which is only exempt from these taxes in particular circumstances. Exemption under section 360 is only available on application to the Inland Revenue. In the case of charities that are registered with the Charity Commission relief will invariably be granted, provided, of course, that the funds of the charity are still being spent for charitable purposes.

Stamp Duty

Generally speaking duty at the rate of up to 2% of the market value of property is charged when it is transferred. However, where the transfer is to a charity, stamp duty is no longer payable but an exemption stamp must be obtained. If you are setting up a new charity, it is easier to gain exemption from stamp duty on the purchase of property or a lease if you acquire charitable status for your organisation before it makes the purchase.

Capital Transfer Tax

The Finance Act 1975 exempts charities from paying capital transfer tax provided any condition attached to the gift is satisfied within twelve months of the transfer. Gifts to a few other organisations are also exempt under schedule 6 of the act. See also page 61.

Capital Gains Tax

By virtue of the Finance Acts 1965 and 1972 this tax is not payable by charities if the gain accruing to the charity is applied for charitable purposes. See page 62. As with CTT a few other bodies are also exempt.

Development Land Tax

This tax is usually chargeable where the development value of land is realised but from March 1982 this tax no longer applies to charities.

Value Added Tax (VAT)

The only special relief for charities is that sales in charity shops etc. of donated goods are zero rated, if the charity is established for the relief of poverty or distress. Non-business supplies are anyway outside the tax, unless they are exported when they will be zero rated. Charities with taxable supplies (i.e. goods and services supplied by them for which they charge) of more than £17,000 a year or £6,000 a quarter must register for VAT but those with less neither have to register nor charge VAT on taxable supplies. Each branch of a charity may be able to be treated as a separate taxable entity. Further information is available from your local VAT Inspector at Customs and Excise or from NCVO and in *Charities and Voluntary Organisations – The Honorary Treasurer.*

National Insurance Surcharge

Under section 57 of the Finance Act 1977 charities are exempted from payment of the surcharge element of National Insurance contributions. You can obtain advice and the scale of contributions for charities (Table CF 398) from your local DHSS office.

Rate relief

As explained on page 2 charities are entitled to receive mandatory relief of 50% of the rates on premises occupied by them and used wholly or mainly for charitable purposes. The rating authorities, in addition, have the discretion to allow relief on such part of the remaining 50% as they think fit.

To obtain this relief you apply under section 40 of the General Rate Act 1967 if you are in England or Wales, or section 4 of the Local Government (Financial Provisions etc.) (Scotland) Act 1962 if you are in Scotland. Forms are available from your rating authority and advice can be obtained from established charities in your area. A visit to the rating department to explain your activities is also likely to help your application for discretionary relief.

It was determined by the Rating (Charity Shops) Act 1976 that a charity shop is entitled to this rate relief but only if it is used wholly or mainly for the sale of goods donated to the charity and the proceeds of sale (after any deduction of expenses) are applied for the purposes of a charity. This is a specific and limited relief. It does not extend, for example, to the administrative offices of the trading arm of a charity, or to the extent to which the shop sells bought-in (as compared with donated) goods.

Following the Rates (Northern Ireland) Order 1977 premises in Northern Ireland are exempt from rates if occupied by a charity and used wholly or mainly for charitable purposes (whether of that charity or of that and other charities). To claim this exemption you should apply under section 41c of the Order to your local rating office or to the Rating Division of the Northern Ireland Department of Finance, see Useful Organisations. Under other parts of section 41 exemption in Northern Ireland is extended beyond charities as such, and there is a move to extend this exemption further.

The Rating (Disabled Persons) Act 1978 requires rating authorities to grant rebates on rates chargeable on properties having special facilities for disabled people or on properties occupied by institutions having the care of the disabled. The word "disabled" is widely defined to include:

    (a)   the provision of residential accommodation for the care of persons suffering from illness or the after care of persons who have been suffering from illness;

    (b)   the provision of facilities for training or keeping suitably occupied persons suffering from illness or persons who have been suffering from illness;

    (c)   the provision of welfare services for disabled persons.

Illness is defined as including any mental disorder and any injury or disability requiring medical or dental treatment or nursing; it seems that blindness by itself is not an illness within the definition. The rebate in question is a total rebate of all the rates payable in respect of the premises occupied for the approved purposes.

Useful Organisations

Artlaw

Artlaw was set up in 1978 to meet the legal needs of visual artists, artist-craftsmen and art organisations in England and Wales. Artlaw Services offer legal advice, conferences, publications, research, insurance and arbitration services. Subscription is open to organisations and individuals.

Artlaw, 358 Strand, London WC2. Telephone 01 240 0610

Arts Council of Great Britain

The Arts Council is primarily an independent body set up to distribute government money for the arts. Their Finance Department can provide model constitutions for arts groups, which have been agreed by the Charity Commission.

Finance Director, Arts Council of Great Britain, 105 Piccadilly, London W1V 0AU. Telephone 01 629 9495

The Charities Aid Foundation

A charity set up in 1924 to encourage and promote the flow of funds to charity, it currently distributes over £8 million each year.

Advice is available on many aspects of charitable giving and fund-raising such as taxation and charity law and up-to-date information on grant-making trusts. CAF also provides a covenant service for individuals and companies which ensures that the maximum advantage is taken of tax concessions without any charge to the donor. They have facilities for setting up trusts and settlements and can act as guardian of capital transferred for charitable use. Additionally, the Foundation operates a computerised covenant administration service for charities.

Annually they publish the invaluable Directory of Grant-Making Trusts and a rather expensive report entitled Charity Statistics. Periodically they hold seminars on related topics.

The Charities Aid Foundation, 48 Pembury Road, Tonbridge, Kent TN9 2JD. Telephone Tonbridge 356323

Charities Branch, Northern Ireland Department of Finance

Organisations wishing to claim charitable privileges and located in Northern Ireland should contact this department for advice. There is no register of Northern Ireland charities.

Charities Branch, Department of Finance, Rosepark House, Upper Newtownards Road, Belfast BT4 3NR. Telephone 023 18 4585

Rating Division, Londonderry House, Chichester Street, Belfast. Telephone 0232 234898

Charities Information Bureau

An innovative organisation being developed by the Birmingham Voluntary Service Council covering Birmingham and the West Midlands only. For those seeking funds it supplies information on appropriate sources and how to apply to them. For those distributing funds it supplies information on organisations seeking funds. It will also provide advice on managing money and book-keeping.

Charities Information Bureau, 161 Corporation Street, Birmingham B4 6PT. Telephone 021 236 1264

The Charity Commission for England and Wales

The Charities Act 1960 describes the general function of the Charity Commission as 'promoting the effective use of charitable resources by encouraging the development of better methods of administration, by giving charity trustees information or advice on any matter affecting the charity and by investigating and checking abuses'. The specific functions of the Charity Commission are exercised more frequently than these general functions. We shall only describe the more important functions briefly. For fuller information consult their leaflets listed under Further Reading.

The Commission, bar the Register, is a somewhat impenetrable organisation. Its Annual Report is an invaluable public guide to its recent actions and can be obtained from HMSO. The staff of around 300 is split between 3 offices. Currently there are three Commissioners, a number of Deputy Commissioners and around 16 Assistant Commissioners.

Throughout this book we have stressed the importance of consulting the Charity Commission on whether or not a draft constitution (governing instrument) is charitable. If the Commission is satisfied that the organisation will be exclusively charitable in its actions, they will often offer free advice on how its governing instrument might be varied to declare purposes which are exclusively charitable. You can request an interview if you think this would help in this process.

The Charity Commission maintains a Register of Charities which the public may consult. As well as being filed alphabetically and by area the slips are filed by type of charity, thus allowing a reader to look up the purposes of various charities and learn how to contact them, and sometimes their approximate income. This is useful both when drawing up an objects clause and when fund-raising. Two complete indexes are kept, one in London and one in Liverpool. In addition there are nine provincial indexes of national charities and most local authorities keep registers of their local charities.

Copies of governing instruments and the accounts of charities may be obtained for a small charge by applying to the Central Register of Charities in London or Liverpool.

Many of the other specific functions of the Charity Commission are described in chapter 6.

Official Custodian for Charities

The Official Custodian can be asked to act as a custodian trustee for a charity. He will then ensure the safe keeping of securities transferred to him and remit the income without deduction of income tax and without charge.

Through the Official Custodian, charities can also invest in the Charities Official Investment Fund.

Addresses

Southern Office:
Charity Commission
14 Ryder Street
St. James's
London SW1Y 6AH
Telephone 01 214 6000

Northern Office (covering charities located north of a line from the Wash to the Bristol Channel)
Charity Commission
Graeme House
Derby Square
Liverpool L2 7SB
Telephone 051 227 3191

Central Register (open Mon-Fri, 10 until 4)
Charity Commission
St Alban's House
57/60 Haymarket
London SW1Y 4QX
Telephone 01 214 6000

Provincial registers are available at:
Reference Library (Birmingham Central Library)
Paradise Circus
Birmingham B3 BHQ
Telephone 021 235 4531

City Treasurer's Dept.
Town Hall
Manchester M60 2JR
Telephone 061 236 3377 ext 2627

City Archives (Room 221)
The Council House
College Green
Bristol BS1 5TR
Telephone Bristol 26031 ext 440

County Secretary's Dept.
Norwich County Council
County Hall
Martineau Lane
Norwich
Norfolk NO1 2DH
Telephone Norwich 611122

County Secretary's Dept.
Northumberland County Council
County Hall
Newcastle-upon-Tyne NE1 1SA
Telephone Newcastle-upon-Tyne 24593

Reference Library
Museum Street
York
Telephone York 55631

Administrative & Legal Services Dept.
Shire Hall
Mold
Clwyd
Telephone Mold 2121 ext 424

Charities Aid Foundation
48 Pembury Road
Tonbridge
Kent TN9 2JD
Telephone Tonbridge 356323

Information Office
Council of Social Service of Wales
Crescent Road
Caerphilly
Mid Glamorgan CF8 1XL
Telephone Caerphilly 869224

Charity Law Reform Committee

The Charity Law Reform Committee was formed in 1972 to press for the reform of certain aspects of charity law and procedures.

Charity Law Reform Committee, Boddington East, Hale Lane, Wendover, Bucks.

Civic Trust

A charity founded in 1957 to encourage improvement of public amenities, civic pride and higher standards of architecture and town planning. Active at both a national and local level. Groups committed to improving a local environment can register with the Civic Trust. Such groups and local history groups can obtain a model charitable constitution and guidance in registering as a charity.

Civic Trust, 17 Carlton House Terrace, London SW1Y 5AW. Telephone 01 930 0914

Commission for Racial Equality

On occasion the Legal Advisors of the CRE are able to offer advice to relevant organisations wishing to register as charities.

Commission for Racial Equality, Elliot House, 10/12 Allington Street, London SW1E 5EH. Telephone 01 828 7022

Inland Revenue Claims Branch

The Charity Division of the Claims Branch consider claims for tax exemption under section 360 of the Income and Corporation Taxes Act 1970. They will also advise promoters of charities during setting up procedures especially if the applicant falls outside the remit of the Charity Commission.

England, Wales and Northern Ireland: Charities Division, Inland Revenue Claims Branch, Magdalen House, Stanley Precinct, Bootle, Lancs L69 9BB. Telephone 051 922 6363

Scotland: Inland Revenue Claims Branch, Trinity Park House, South Trinity Road, Edinburgh EH5 3SD. Telephone 031 552 6255

Inter-Action Advisory Service

A division of Inter-Action Trust Ltd which provides advice and guidance to community groups and voluntary organisations. Advice is available on financial management, charitable registration, organisational matters and a host of other topics. All 12 part-time advisors spend the other part of their time as practitioners in the field. Currently much of the advice is provided at a nominal charge

Inter-Action also has a specialist architecture service for voluntary organisations, known as Neighbourhood Use of Building Space. (N.U.B.S.)

Inter-Action Advisory Service, 15 Wilkin Street, London NW5 3NG. Telephone 01 267 9421

Legislation-Monitoring Service for Charities

Set up in 1978 this service provides the following assistance to members:
- drawing the attention of members to current legislation and proposed legislation as it may affect charities
- circulating information amongst participating charities and voluntary organisations
- on occasions coordinating concerted action on behalf of members

The annual subscription in 1979 was £27. If you are not sure whether to join ask for a specimen Quarterly Report or Circular.

Correspondence address: Mr Harry Kidd, Legislation-Monitoring Service for Charities, St John's College, Oxford OX1 3JP. Telephone Oxford 47671 ext 244

The National Council for Voluntary Organisations

Amongst the services offered by the NCVO to voluntary organisations is advice on legal matters. Their Legal Department is available to help existing or potential organisations on legal matters from employment to lotteries and gaming. They are particularly well informed on charity law and the registration of charities.

The NCVO News Service publication carries articles on changes in law which have a bearing on the activities of charities. Other departments and affiliated organisations specialise in matters relevant to MSC employment projects (Community Service Unit), employment workshops and community associations. Their publishing imprint, Bedford Square Press, produces a range of useful titles.

National Council for Voluntary Organisations, 26 Bedford Square, London WC1B 3HU. Telephone 01 636 4066

National Federation of Housing Associations

The National Federation is the central organisation for advising and co-ordinating housing associations and making representations on their behalf.

The Federation will undertake the registration of housing associations and can provide model rules. Their model H.13 1977 establishes a housing association as an Industrial and Provident Society having charitable status.

England and Wales: National Federation of Housing Associations, 30/32 Southampton Street, London WC2E 7HE. Telephone 01 240 2771

Scotland: Scottish Federation of Housing Associations, 42 York Place, Edinburgh EH1 3HU. Telephone 031 556 1435

Northern Ireland: Northern Ireland Federation of Housing Associations, 123 York Street, Belfast BT15 1AB. Telephone 0232 230446

Registry of Friendly Societies

This Registry is responsible both for Friendly Societies and for Industrial and Provident Societies. Amongst its major functions are:
- to register the rules of new societies and changes made to them
- to maintain a public record file of societies and their annual returns
- to hear and determine disputes referred for arbitration

Registry of Friendly Societies, 17 North Audley Street, London W1Y 2AP. Telephone 01 629 7001

Scottish Council of Social Service

The SCSS is an independent voluntary organisation working throughout Scotland for the development of voluntary action. They can provide advice to Scottish groups when they are setting up as charities. See Constitutions Workpack under Further Reading.

SCSS, 18/19 Claremont Crescent, Edinburgh EH7 4QD. Telephone 031 556 3882

The Working Party of Landed Charities

The principal objects of the Working Party are to provide in respect of the investment land of charities a service similar to that provided on other matters by the Legislation-Monitoring Service for Charities (see above); and to provide for the exchange of views and information between landed charities on matters which affect their real property, both urban and rural.

The annual subscription in 1979 is £25 for individual charities and £100 for collective organisations of charities.

Correspondence address: Mr H Kidd, The Working Party of Landed Charities, St John's College, Oxford OX1 3JP. Telephone Oxford 47671 ext 244

Further Reading

This is a selection of books, pamphlets and articles covering various related topics. Most of the expensive ones will be available through your public library.

'Campaigning & Charitable Status: How Far You Can Go' by Elizabeth Cairns in *Campaigning and Lobbying*. Available from Directory of Social Change, 9 Mansfield Place, London NW3. A useful piece by a former Assistant Charity Commissioner.

Charitable Giving and Taxation by the Charitable Giving and Taxation Consultants. Available from Craigmyle & Co. Ltd., The Grove, Harpenden, Herts, £7.50.

Charities by Benedict Nightingale, 1973, Allen Lane.

Charities Act, 1960, 8 & 9 ELIZ. 2. CH. 58., HMSO, 47p.

Charities Act (Northern Ireland) 1964, CH 33, HMSO, 60p.

Charities for the Relief of the Poor and Charities for the Relief of Sickness. Two free leaflets issued as guidance by the Charity Commission in 1978.

Charities' Guide to the Community Land Act 1975 and the Development Land Tax Act 1976, 18 pages, NCSS.

Charities, Trusts and Social Welfare by Michael Chesterman, 512 pages, 1979, Weidenfeld & Nicolson, paperback about £10, cased about £17.50. A book for students that examines the English law of charity in its social and economic context and against its historical background.

Charities and Voluntary Organisations – The Honorary Treasurer by Lawrence S Fenton, 50 pages, 1980, Institute of Chartered Accountants.

The Charity Commissioners: How They Can Help Charity Trustees. A free booklet available from the Charity Commission.

Charity Law and Voluntary Organisations: Report of the Goodman Committee, 150 pages, 1976, Bedford Square Press. The status of this report is currently unclear. It is the outcome of an independent committee of inquiry set up by the NCSS to examine the effect of charity law and practice on voluntary organisations. Useful as a guide on aspects of Charity Commission practice, it now appears to be gaining a certain prescriptive status.

Charity Trustees' Guide: An NCSS Handbook by A R Longley, Martin Dockray, Jacqueline Sallon, 1979, Bedford Square Press, 32 pages, £1.25.

'Community Organisation: Forms of Organisation' by Harry Rajak in the *Legal Action Group Bulletin*, June 1977. Useful analysis of the pros and cons of incorporated and unincorporated legal formats.

'Community Organisations: The Mysteries of Charitable Status' by Harry Rajak in the *Legal Action Bulletin* November 1978. Mainly on setting up law centres and other advice agencies.

Constitutions Workpack. Published in 1978 by the Scottish Council of Social Service at £1.50. Available from SCSS, 18/19 Claremont Crescent, Edinburgh, EH7 4QD. Succinct and particularly useful for community associations.

Directory of Grant-Making Trusts edited by Elizabeth Skinner. Published annually by the Charities Aid Foundation, 48 Pembury Road, Tonbridge, Kent TN9 2JD. An invaluable guide for any charity that is looking for grant assistance. It explains how to apply for money and from whom. Available in many public libraries or direct from CAF at £35.

Every Penny Counts: A Review of Investment Opportunities and Asset Management for Charities, 56 pages, 1975, Charities Aid Foundation, 75p direct from CAF.

A Guide for Charity Trustees by C P Hill, 156 pages, 1966, Faber and Faber. C P Hill was a Charity Commissioner.

Investment Management by Charity Trustees. A free leaflet issued by the Charity Commission which offers advice on investment policies suitable for charities.

Law Relating to Charities by D G Cracknell, 255 pages, 1973, Oyez. A legal textbook but shorter and more recent than *Tudor on Charities*.

The Law and Practise Relating to Charities by H Picarda, 1977, Butterworth. At £45 this is best consulted in a library.

Legal Frameworks Handbook for Communes and Collectives, 40 pages, 1975, 55p. Available from Laurieston Hall, Castle Douglas, Kirkcudbrightshire.

Lotteries and Gaming: Voluntary Organisations and the Law, 40 pages, 1978, 65p, Bedford Square Press of the NCSS.

The Modern Law of Charities by G W Keeton and L A Sheriden, 2nd edition, 1971, Queens University Faculty of Law.

The Registration of Charities by John Michael Fryer. A Master of Law thesis submitted in 1976, 513 pages, available from the University of Warwick library and the National Lending Library. A very thorough appraisal.

The Official Custodian for Charities: Charity Funds. A free booklet from the Charity Commission.

The Official Custodian for Charities: Charity Land. A free booklet from the Charity Commission.

Rating (Charity Shops) Act 1976, c.45, HMSO, 8p.

Report of the Charity Commissioners for England and Wales. Published annually, HMSO, about £1.35.

Responsibilities of Charity Trustees. A free booklet available from the Charity Commission.

Trusts and Trustees: Cases and Materials by R H Maudsley and E H Burn, 672 pages, Butterworths, 1972. The 150 pages on charities is much more readable than most books on the topic and describes some interesting cases.

Trustee Investment Act, 1961. 9 & 10 ELIZ. 2. CH.62. HMSO, 45p.

Tudor on Charities by Douglas H McMullen and others, 6th edition, 755 pages, 1967, Sweet and Maxwell. The standard work on charity law. Not suitable for readers without legal training.

Workers' Co-operatives – A Handbook by Peter Cockerton, Tim Gilmour-White, John Pearce, Anna Whyatt, due 1980, Aberdeen People's Press with the Authors, about 90 pages, about £5 and £1.75.

Index

77

High Court, 25
hospitals, 50
House of Lords, 25, 46-47, 48
housing, 17, 48
humanism, 12
Income and Corporation Taxes Act
    section 360, 64
income tax, 58-59, 64, see also
    covenant
incorporated organisations, 26-35
    definition, 26-27, 30
Industrial and Provident Society, xii,
    22, 26-35
    advantages and disadvantages,
        34-35
    definition, 33
    tax relief, 35
industry, as charitable, 13, 19
Inland Revenue, xiii, 6, **23-24**, 33, 48,
    51, 59, 58-66, **71**
Inter-Action Advisory Service, 72
investment of charity money, 37, 43
    in trading company, 53-57
job creation projects, 19-20
land, 43
    development land tax, 62, 64
    Working Party of Landed
        Charities, 73
law centres, 18
legal formats, xii, 26-35
Legislation – Monitoring Service for
    Charities, 72
liability, 27, 30, 31
    limited, 32
    of trading company, 53
library, 10
limited company, 26-35
    advantages and disadvantages, 32,
        34
    definition, 30-31
    Model Constitution, 32
    stationery, 45
loans
    by charities, 43, 56
    to charities, 43
Local Government (Financial
    Provisions etc.) (Scotland)
    Act 1962, 65

Macnaghten, Lord, 6
mail-order selling, 53
management, 43, see also *trustees*
    delegation, financial manage-
    ment, constitution
Manpower Service Commission
    (MSC), 19-20
means-tests, 18
medicine, 18
members of a company, 36
    duties, 36
    number required, 31, 34
    powers of, 30, 36, 44
members of an Industrial and
    Provident Society, 34, 36
Memorandum, of company, 31
mental illness, 8
moral welfare, 13
museums, 50
mutual-aid groups, 17
National Council for Civil Liberties,
    48
National Council of Social Service, 20,
    72
National Federation of Community
    Associations, 17
National Federation of Housing
    Associations, 18, 73
National Insurance, relief from
    surcharge, 65
Neighbourhood Use of Buildings and
    Space (NUBS), 72
non-resident, tax relief, 62
Northern Ireland, xii, **23**
Northern Ireland Department of
    Finance, 23, 68
    Rating Division, 66
Northern Ireland Federation of
    Housing Associations, 73
nuns, 12
objects clause, **35**
    changes to, 29, 37
    models, 9, 12, 13, 15, 20, 21, 36
Official Custodian for Charities, 69
osteopathy, 18
other purposes as charitable, 13-14
overdraft, 43 see also *accounts* and
    loans

Inter-Action

Inter-Action is the umbrella name for Inter-Action Trust Limited and its nine associated charitable companies and trusts. Founded in 1968 by Ed Berman to stimulate community involvement and to experiment with uses of creativity, it is now based in the London Borough of Camden.

Inter-Action can provide voluntary organisations, charities, schools, community groups and others with a range of services. Some of these facilities are available to local authorities and commercial users if there is down-time.

For more information about any of these facilities please contact the listed person at Inter-Action. For further general information about Inter-Action please contact our Publicity Person.

Inter-Action Trust Ltd
15 Wilkin Street
London NW5 3NX

Telephone 01 267 9421 (6 lines) or 01 485 0881 (3 lines).

81

Media and design services

Video and audio equipment and studios (both static and mobile) are available for hire. Contact the Audio-visual Department.

A freelance photographer can cover your events and a set of display stands are available for exhibitions. Contact the Photographer at Inter-Action.

The Inter-Action Design Department is able to undertake design work for leaflets, books, displays, and much else. Or you may like to hire a badge making machine.

A process camera (Agfa 2001) is available for use by arrangement. Contact the Design Department at Inter-Action.

Architectural services

Inter-Action's architects provide specialist services to voluntary organisations and local authorities. Contact the Neighbourhood Use of Buildings and Space at Inter-Action.

Country Wings

This new department will assist youth and community groups develop bases in the countryside. Contact the Country Wings Administrator.

Training

Training is available in the community arts and in the Inter-Action Game Method and other community and drama skills. Contact the Training Officer at Inter-Action.

Rehearsal and meeting rooms and hall

To hire these contact the Centre Manager at Inter-Action.

Children's and community theatre troupe

Inter-Action's theatre troupe tours schools, playgroups, playgrounds, pensioners clubs and many other venues. Projects in repertoire include the Animobile (an unusual farmyard-on-wheels), the Dolls Show for Under-Fives and Community Cameos. If you would like details of any of these projects contact the Dogg's Troupe Administrator at Inter-Action.

General Advisory Service

Fourteen advisors offer consultancy on a wide variety of topics of interest to voluntary organisations from financial management to charitable registration. Contact Advisory Service Co-ordinator at Inter-Action.

Publishing

We offer publishing services to charities and other voluntary organisations. Contact our Publisher.

Community and education

Our community and education work is mainly in Greater London and particularly the Borough of Camden. It includes Kentish Town City Farm, an alternative education project, an adventure soft-room for under 5s, community resource facilities and much else. Contact the Camden Team at Inter-Action.

Research

Through our Institute for Social Enterprise we can undertake action-research contracts in the UK and abroad, alongside our own research in the field. Contact the Director of the International Institute for Social Enterprise at Inter-Action.

Computer room

We can sometimes offer computer and wordprocessing facilities through our Computer Manager.

Kentish Town City Farm

An education and youth work project which is often open to the public. Contact the City Farm Manager, 1 Cressfield Close, Grafton Road, London NW5. Telephone 01 485 4585.

Employment workshop

The Kirklees Youth Training Workshop undertakes manufacturing and distribution work within certain criteria. The fields covered include carpentry, metalwork, sewing, book distribution and clerical work. For further information contact the Director, Inter-Action North, 2 Hawkesby Court, New Street, Huddersfield. Telephone 0484 44239.